D0194833

THE EXECUTIVE'S ALMANAC

Copyright © 2006 by Milton Moskowitz

All rights reserved. No part of this book may be reproduced in any form without written permission from the publisher.

Library of Congress Cataloging in Publication Number: 2005910828

ISBN 1-59474-101-8
Printed in China
Typeset in Century and Trade Gothic

Designed by Doogie Horner
Illustrations by Kevin Sprouls

Distributed in North America by Chronicle Books
85 Second Street
San Francisco, CA 94105

10 9 8 7 6 5 4 3 2 1

Quirk Books
215 Church Street
Philadelphia, PA 19106
www.quirkbooks.com

THE EXECUTIVE'S ALMANAC

A Diverse Portfolio of Eclectic Business Trivia

By Milton Moskowitz

QUIRK BOOKS
PHILADELPHIA

INTRODUCTION

First of all, what this book is not:

It's not a guide to becoming rich.
It's not a guide on how to run a business.
It's not a guide to advancing in the company.
It's not a guide to finding the best stocks to buy.

This is not to say that any or all of these goals could not be achieved by reading this book. It's possible. But those would be incidental outcomes. The thrust of this little volume is neither mercenary nor practical. It's more in the realm of fact-based entertainment.

In writing about business for 50 years, I have always been fascinated by the odd things that go on, the stories of how companies were born and how they died, pompous statements by CEOs, quirky lists, invidious comparisons, internecine quarrels, soaring—and plunging—stock prices, and attempts to introduce social responsibility into a landscape dominated by money.

This is a book, then, to be read at the beach or at bars or in the bathroom or while looking at the stock tables or watching *Seinfeld* reruns. It's a combination reference book, *Jeopardy!* source, and trivia collection. It does not purport to be comprehensive. There are a lot of other facts out there. Send them in. We'll try to get them in the next edition.

Meanwhile, enjoy.

—Milton Moskowitz

Best Perks in U.S. Business

Fannie Mae	$22,000 in subsidies to help employees buy a home.
SAS Institute	$300-a-month charge for full-time child care.
MBNA	Four-year college scholarships for children and grandchildren of employees.
Autodesk	Six-week paid sabbaticals every four years.
Northwestern Mutual	Sumptuous free lunch every day.
American Cast Iron Pipe	On-site medical and dental care for all employees and retirees, for the rest of their lives.

WHATEVER HAPPENED TO . . .

RCA

— FOUNDED 1919 —

Sold to General Electric (GE) for $6.3 billion in 1985 and then dismembered. NBC remained with GE. RCA television sets are now made by a Chinese company, TCL (see page 88). GE stripped the RCA name from the 30 Rockefeller Plaza building in Rockefeller Center and renamed it the GE building.

In 2005, Nicole Kidman made it into the fiftieth anniversary edition of the *Guinness World Records* after becoming the highest-paid actress in a commercial. Kidman appeared in a four-minute TV commercial for Chanel No. 5, directed by Baz Luhrmann (he also directed her in *Moulin Rouge*). For this gig, Kidman was paid more than $3.7 million, or $928,800 per minute.

Nicole Kidman

Creative Stock Market Ticker Symbols

LUV	Southwest Airlines
ROCK	Gibraltar Industries (steel)
ZEUS	Olympic Steel
NUT	Mauna Loa
BID	Sotheby's
LENS	Concord Camera
XRAY	Dentsply
OO	Oakley
VO	Seagram
SUIT	Men's Wearhouse
HAMS	Smithfield Foods
BEN	Franklin Resources
CAKE	Cheesecake Factory
DISH	EchoStar
EAT	Brinker International
FUN	Cedar Fair
LOOK	Looksmart
DNA	Genentech

Pfizer's Blockbuster Array of Drugs

Few companies are as candid as Pfizer Inc. in disclosing sales figures for their products. In its 2004 annual report, the world's largest pharmaceutical company presented this summary of its top 21 prescription drugs, which account for sales of more than $37 billion. Pfizer's total sales in 2004: $52.5 billion.

DRUG	USE	2004 SALES
1. Lipitor	cholesterol reducer	$10.86 billion
2. Norvasc	antihypertension agent	$4.46 billion
3. Zoloft	antidepressant	$3.36 billion
4. Celebrex	pain reliever for arthritis sufferers	$3.3 billion
5. Neurontin	treatment for epilepsy and neuropathic pain	$2.72 billion
6. Zithromax	world's bestselling antibiotic	$1.85 billion
7. Viagra	for erectile dysfunction	$1.68 billion
8. Bextra	for relief of arthritis pain	$1.29 billion
9. Zyrtec	antihistamine	$1.29 billion
10. Xalatan	world's bestselling drug for intraocular pressure	$1.23 billion
11. Diflucan	antifungal agent	$945 million
12. Detrol	bestselling medicine for overactive bladder	$904 million
13. Genotropin	human growth hormone	$736 million

DRUG	USE	2004 SALES
14. Campto/ Camptosar	treatment for metastatic colorectal cancer	$554 million
15. Geodon/ Zeldox	antipsychotic	$467 million
16. Zyvox	treatment for infections caused by drug-resistant bacteria	$463 million
17. Aricept	leading drug in the Alzheimer's disease market	$308 million
18. Vfend	antifungal drug	$287 million
19. Relpax	treatment for migraine headaches	$169 million
20. Aromasin	aromatase inhibitor, reducing risk of breast cancer recurrence	$143 million
21. Caduet	combination of Lipitor and Norvasc to treat hypertension and high cholesterol in one pill	$50 million

Junk bond king Michael Milken made $124 million in 1984, $135 million in 1985, $294 million in 1986, $550 million in 1987, and $750 million in 1988. After serving 22 months in prison for securities fraud and paying settlements totaling $900 million, he emerged as the leading funder of prostate cancer research (he is a prostate cancer survivor). *Forbes* estimates his worth at $1 billion. Companies in which he holds major stakes include Knowledge Universe Learning Corp. (child care centers), Nobel Learning Communities (private schools), and LeapFrog (educational toys).

Michael Milken

Soichiro Honda

a Japanese Original

SOICHIRO HONDA, founder of the Honda Motor Company, defied all the stereotypes of uptight Japanese businessmen. Sometimes called the "Henry Ford of Japan," he built motorcycles and speedboats before manufacturing automobiles. And he was a bit of a carouser, as he described himself in his autobiography, *Honda and His Machines*. He spent World War II making piston rings. At the end of the war, when he was 39, he sold his business and settled down to a year of serious drinking and playing the *shakuhachi*, a bamboo flute. He bought a barrel of pure alcohol, watered it down a bit, and hosted drinking parties. In an interview with the Japanese theatrical director Keita Asari, he described what happened next:

Soichiro Honda

> My wife was going out on her bicycle to buy black market rice. But she couldn't find any in the area. She got mad and said to me, "For once, you try going out and buying the rice." No way did I want to do that, so I picked up a little motor, something the army must have thrown away, and I hooked it up to the bicycle for her. I make it sound simple, but putting that motor on the bike took some doing. To make a gas tank I needed a sheet of steel. But ordinary steel would rust and get into the gasoline, so I really wanted tin plating. But with

> the controls on the economy, tin-plated steel was hard to come by. So I went to this night market and bought a hot water bottle—the kind you use as a bed warmer—and made it into a gas tank.

That was the genesis of the Honda motorcycle, the first product made by Honda Motor. By 1968, Honda had sold one million motorcycles in the United States. With no support or encouragement from the Japanese government, which felt Japan already had enough automakers, Soichiro Honda next began making cars, scoring his first major triumph in 1972 with the Honda Civic, powered by a vortex-controlled combustion engine that helped to solve the pollution problem by producing clean exhaust without the addition of a catalytic converter. The Civic was followed by the Accord in 1976, identified by automotive writer Brock Yates as a "milestone automobile" because it showed that the Japanese were "capable of mass-producing automobiles that rivaled the quality once considered to be the exclusive province of Mercedes-Benz, BMW, and Porsche."

In 1973, when he was 66 years old and his company was riding high, Soichiro Honda stepped down from the day-to-day management of Honda Motor. In an interview with writer Mitz Noda, he explained why:

> I lost my sex power. I don't say I have lost all my sex power, but I must admit frequency of doing and recovery has not been the same as when I was young. Great leaders love sex, and I am not a great leader anymore. I can't drink anymore. Two cups of sake is enough. For entertaining customers and employees, presidents should be able to drink more. I know what I can't do. I have no willingness to learn new technology anymore. Without sex power, drinking habits, and work desire, I should quit the life of an entrepreneur.

Soichiro Honda died in 1992 at age 86.

Ratio of CEO Pay to Average Worker Pay

Average worker pay in 2004:	**$528** a week
Average CEO pay in 2004:	**$226,923** a week
	Ratio: 431 to 1

From 1990 to 2004*

CEO pay increased 319%

S&P 500 average rose 238%

Corporate profits increased 87%

Average worker pay rose 5%

* *Figures adjusted for inflation*

If America's national minimum wage had gone up as much as CEO pay since 1990, it would stand today at $23.03 an hour, four times the current minimum of $5.15 an hour.

Golden Age of Film

	1946	2004
U.S. Population	141 million	295 million
Number of Movie Screens	19,000	36,000
Weekly Attendance	100 million	25 million

PROFILE

Koch Industries

MOST PEOPLE HAVE NEVER HEARD of Kansas-based Koch Industries because the company is privately held, with no stock market listing, and it makes very few consumer products. Residents of the upper Midwest states might recognize one of its brands, Blue Planet gasoline. But make no mistake, Koch Industries is enormous, with annual sales estimated at $40 billion and 30,000 employees. The company that started out as an oil refiner now operates more than a dozen businesses:

- Forest Hills Resources in Corpus Christi, Texas, produces 1 billion pounds (454 million kg) of paraxylene a year, a plastic used in beverage containers, automobile parts, and clothing.
- TrueNorth Energy, miner of oil sands in Alberta, Canada, produces 95,000 barrels of bitumen a day.
- Koch Pipeline operates 13,000 miles (21,000 km) of pipeline carrying crude oil, natural gas liquids, and anhydrous ammonia.
- Koch Hydrocarbon processes and transports 25 percent of the total natural gas liquids produced in the United States.
- KoSa B.V. is one of the world's largest producers of polyester.
- Koch Materials sells enough asphalt every year to pave 125,000 miles (200,000 km) of roads. It has plants around the world.
- Matador Cattle Company runs 15,000 head of cattle over 380,000 acres (1500 sq km)—and it employs 25 cowboys.

At the end of 2005, Koch Industries signed a deal to acquire the big wood products company Georgia-Pacific, which owns Brawny paper towels and Dixie Cups, among other goods. The deal was for $13.2 billion—in cash. This made Koch America's largest privately owned company, displacing Cargill.

The annual meeting of the Chubb Corp. on April 25, 2000, at its headquarters in Warren, New Jersey, was the shortest ever annual meeting of a U.S. company (and maybe of any company in the world). Elapsed time: 9 minutes, 36 seconds.

Average Age of U.S. Car Owners

Make	Age	Make	Age
Buick	62	Ford	45
Mercury	59	Audi	44
Lincoln	56	BMW	44
Cadillac	54	Honda	44
Jaguar	54	Infiniti	44
Lexus	51	Saab	44
Chrysler	49	Acura	43
Mercedes-Benz	49	Nissan	42
Toyota	47	Volkswagen	41
Volvo	47		

The study in the 269-room castle of Alfred Krupp, son of the founder of Germany's mighty Krupp steel company, was located over the stables so that he could inhale the enriching smell of horse manure, according to William Manchester, author of the book *The Arms of Krupp.*

Cost of a full-page color advertisement in the U.S. edition of *Sports Illustrated*

$280,000

Cost of the same advertisement in the *Sports Illustrated Swimsuit Edition*

$328,000

(adjusted for increased circulation)

Ascendant China

Ted C. Fishman documents the rise of the Chinese economy in his 2005 book, *China Inc.*:

- From 1982 to 2002, while the U.S. economy was growing at an annual rate of 3.3 percent, China's economy grew at an annual rate of 9.5 percent, meaning it "doubled nearly three times over."
- In 2003 China bought
    - 7 percent of the world's oil.
    - 25 percent of the world's aluminum and steel.
    - nearly 33 percent of the world's iron ore and coal.
    - 40 percent of the world's cement.
- China makes 40 percent of all furniture sold in the United States.
- In the first 10 months of 2003, 3,000 Christmas-decoration factories exported more than $900 million of tree trimmings and plastic Santas.

China leads the world in killing coal miners. In 2004, more than 6,000 deaths were recorded in Chinese mines. In October 2004, a mine explosion killed 148 miners, and in November 2004, a blast killed 166 miners in the northern province of Shaanxi. In February 2005, more than 200 miners died after a gas explosion in a mine at Fuxin in northeast China. The blast occurred 794 feet (240 m) underground.

THE J.M. SMUCKER COMPANY, AMERICA'S LARGEST PRODUCER OF JAMS, JELLIES, AND PRESERVES, WAS FOUNDED IN 1897 BY JEROME M. SMUCKER, WHO WAS A STRICT MENNONITE. THE FAMILY'S ORIGINAL NAME WAS "SMOKER," BUT BECAUSE HE WAS AGAINST SMOKING, JEROME'S FATHER CHANGED IT TO "SMUCKER."

The Altoids Saga

ALTOIDS ARE A BRAND of breath mints—available in peppermint, wintergreen, spearmint, cinnamon, ginger, and licorice flavors—whose history goes back to England at the end of the eighteenth century. Every tin carries a legend that reads as follows (with the language varying slightly by the flavor being described):

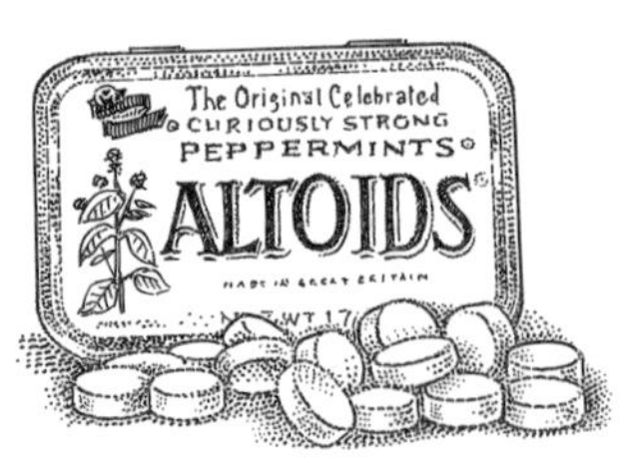

> ALTOIDS, the Original Celebrated Curiously Strong Mints, were first produced in England at the turn of the nineteenth century during the reign of King George III. Smith & Co. (est. 1780), the small London firm which developed the original "curiously strong" recipe, later became part of Callard & Bowser, a prestigious English confectioner founded in 1937. Today, ALTOIDS sweets are made in the same exacting standards as the original ALTOIDS recipe developed more than 200 years ago.

Unmentioned in the legend is the recent history of Altoids. During the 1970s, the English company, then known as Callard & Bowser-Suchard, was acquired by the American conglomerate Beatrice Foods, maker of such goodies as Krispy Kreme doughnuts, La Choy Oriental foods, Fireside marshmallows, and Holloway Milk Duds. Then, in 1982, the company passed into the hands of the English confectionery firm Terry's of York, which was acquired in 1993 by Kraft Foods, a subsidiary of tobacco giant Philip Morris. That ownership held until 2005, when Kraft sold the business to the Wm. Wrigley Jr. Company of Chicago.

Through the years, the tins in which Altoids are packed have found various uses (paper clip holders, pinhole cameras, iPod battery packs), and some of the older versions have become collector's items. During the 1990s, an Internet rumor about Altoids made its way into Kenneth Starr's report on President Bill Clinton's liaison with Monica Lewinsky—Lewinsky was said to have shown the president an e-mail touting Altoids as an aid to oral sex.

Curiously strong mints, indeed.

*Prices of Sought-After First English-Language Editions in the Rare Book Trade**

		Market Value
Dashiell Hammett	*The Maltese Falcon* (1930)	\$85,000–100,000
James Joyce	*Ulysses* (1922)	\$75,000–90,000
Ernest Hemingway	*The Sun Also Rises* (1926)	\$65,000–70,000
William Faulkner	*The Sound and the Fury* (1929)	\$60,000–75,000
Henry Miller	*Tropic of Cancer* (1934)	\$30,000–40,000
J. D. Salinger	*The Catcher in the Rye* (1951)	\$25,000–30,000
Tennessee Williams	*A Streetcar Named Desire* (1947)	\$15,000–20,000
Harper Lee	*To Kill a Mockingbird* (1960)	\$15,000–20,000
Vladimir Nabokov	*Lolita* (1955)	\$10,000–15,000

**Market values based on first editions in their original dust jackets and in mint condition.*

5 U.S. Stocks You Should Have Bought in 1985

Amgen (AMGN), based in Thousand Oaks, California, is the leading maker of biotech drugs.

$1,000 invested in Amgen shares on the first trading day of 1985 would have grown to $558,891 by March 31, 2005.

UnitedHealth Group (UNH), based in Minnetonka, Minnesota, operates a variety of health care plans.

$1,000 invested in UnitedHealth Group shares on the first trading day of 1985 would have grown to $397,516 by March 31, 2005.

Paychex (PAYX), Rochester, New York, handles the payrolls of half a million companies.

$1,000 invested in Paychex shares on the first trading day of 1985 would have grown to $234,287 by March 31, 2005.

Franklin Resources (BEN), based in San Mateo, California, ranks as the fourth largest mutual fund manager.

$1,000 invested in Franklin Resources shares on the first trading day of 1985 would have grown to $230,979 by March 31, 2005.

St. Jude Medical (STJ), St. Paul, Minnesota, is a leading supplier of heart valves and pacemakers.

$1,000 invested in St. Jude shares would have multiplied to $203,604 by March 31, 2005.

5 U.S. Stocks You Should Have Avoided in 1985

Harken Energy (HEC), Southlake, Texas, is an oil and gas producer that bought George W. Bush's failing oil company in 1986. (Bush served on the board from 1986 to 1993.)

$1,000 invested in Harken Energy shares on the first trading day of 1985 would have skidded to $25.29 by March 31, 2005 (when Bush was in the White House).

America West (AWA), based in Tempe, Arizona, was ranked as the eighth largest U.S. airline until its 2005 merger with US Airways.

$1,000 invested in America West shares at the start of 1985 would have declined in value to $70.20 by March 31, 2005.

WebFinancial (WEFN), based in New York, is an online banker offering loans that conform to laws in Utah.

$1,000 invested in WebFinancial shares on the first day of trading in 1985 was worth $131 on March 31, 2005.

Delta Air Lines (DAL), based in Atlanta, is the third largest U.S. airline.

$1,000 invested in Delta shares at the start of 1985 plunged to $229 on March 31, 2005.

USG (USG), based in Chicago, is the world's largest maker of Sheetrock, its tradename for drywall and plasterboard panels.

$1,000 invested in USG at the start of 1985 dropped to $334.87 by March 31, 2005.

Note: Final return assumes that all dividends and distributions were reinvested in stock.

Wal-Mart Trivia

- Excluding automotive sales, about eight cents of every dollar spent in U.S. stores ends up at Wal-Mart.
- Members of more than 80 percent of U.S. households visit a Wal-Mart at least once during the year.
- Wal-Mart's annual sales ($300 billion plus) top those of any other company. They are equal to Switzerland's gross national product.
- In 2004, five of the top ten U.S. billionaires were members of the Walton family.
- Placed side by side, without parking lots, Wal-Mart's 3,500 stores would cover most of Manhattan.
- With more than 1.3 million employees, Wal-Mart is the largest private employer in the United States—and also in Mexico (100,000 employees).
- Procter & Gamble derives 18 percent of its sales from Wal-Mart, Kellogg 12 percent, and Clorox 25 percent.
- If Wal-Mart were a country, it would rank as China's eighth largest trading partner, importing $12 billion of goods annually.
- In 2003, Wal-Mart sold enough Ol'Roy dog biscuits to circle Earth twice.
- Gary Stibel, managing partner of New England Consulting, said: "If we let Wal-Mart negotiate with OPEC, we would be paying $1 a gallon for gasoline."
- $5,000 invested in Wal-Mart stock in 1980 would have grown to $2.5 million by 2005.

FRATRICIDE

The Pritzkers

THIS CHICAGO FAMILY, whose wealth derived from real estate, auto parts, and hotels, among other businesses, was driven apart by dissension in the early years of the twenty-first century. Liesel Pritzker, a 20-year-old actress and student at Columbia University, claimed that her father and other relatives had looted her trust fund. Her elder brother, Matthew, joined her in a suit alleging that $2 billion had been siphoned from her funds. After months of wrangling, the suit was settled out of court, with Liesel and Matthew getting a combined total of $900 million including control of trusts in their names worth $170 million each. The Pritzker holdings are valued at $15 billion.

WORLD'S TOP 10

Automotive Companies*

		Vehicles Sold Worldwide
1.	General Motors	8.2 million
2.	Toyota	7.5 million
3.	Ford	6.8 million
4.	Volkswagen	5.1 million
5.	DaimlerChrysler	4.7 million
6.	Peugeot Citroën	3.4 million
7.	Nissan	3.3 million
8.	Honda	3.2 million
9.	Renault	2.5 million
10.	BMW	1.2 million

**ranked by vehicle sales in 2004*

PROFILE

Tata Group

INDIA'S LARGEST COMMERCIAL ENTERPRISE emerged in the second half of the nineteenth century from the country's small but influential Parsee community. The Parsees are Zoroastrians, a sect named for Zoroaster, a Persian prophet of the sixth century B.C.

Jamsetji Tata, who came from a family of Parsee priests, started a trading company in 1868, when he was twenty-nine, and then set about bringing the Industrial Revolution to India. He built a cotton mill in the central Indian city of Nagpur, opened the luxurious Taj Mahal Hotel in Bombay (the first building in the city to be lit by electricity), and started projects that resulted in hydroelectric power for Bombay and a large steel mill in the jungle village of Jamshedpur in northeastern India. He also put up the seed money for a school that became the Indian Institute of Science at Bangalore, a place renowned now for its graduate engineers (many of them working in Silicon Valley).

Jamsetji Tata

Jamsetji Tata died in 1904, but his work was continued by his family. A member of the Tata family remains at the helm in the twenty-first century—Ratan Tata, nephew of J. R. D. Tata, who led the company for 54 years. The Tata Group was active throughout the twentieth century, starting and developing companies in various fields. Central to their operations was a strong ethical code that demanded respect for all employees—it was this feature that enabled the Tata Group to function well even under socialist governments. In fact, many of the Tata companies were joint ventures in which the government held a major interest.

The Tata Group consists of 32 public companies—among them Tata Motors, Tata Steel, Tata Power, and Tata Chemicals. Tata Motors holds 60 percent of the commercial vehicle market in India, and in 1998 it introduced the first Indian-made automobile, the Indica, followed in 2002 by the Indigo. The Tata Group now has operations in more than 40 countries across six continents. It comprises 91 businesses, with total sales (in 2003 to 2004) of $14 billion. More than 20 percent of its sales come from outside India.

In 2000, Tata spent $475 (£271) million to buy Tetley Tea, a British company with a worldwide brand. This transaction represented the first major world business acquisition by an Indian company.

TOP 10

Beer Brands in the U.S. Market

	Market Share
BUD LIGHT	20.1%
BUDWEISER	14.7%
MILLER LITE	8.9%
COORS LIGHT	7.2%
NATURAL LIGHT	4.2%
BUSCH	3.7%
CORONA EXTRA	3.5%
BUSCH LIGHT	2.7%
MILLER HIGH LIFE	2.5%
HEINEKEN	2.3%

Percent of total market held between the top 10: 69.8%

In the Immortal Words of . . .

In 2005, Trevor Beattie, known as the *enfant terrible* of the British advertising scene, resigned as chairman and creative director of the London office of TBWA Worldwide, taking with him two senior executives, Andrew McGuinness and Bil Bungay, to set up a new agency, Beattie McGuinness Bungay. TBWA is one of the ad agencies in the Omnicom stable, and Beattie had spent more than a decade there. He's responsible for coming up with the acronym FCUK for the fashion retailer French Connection UK. In a 2002 interview with the *Wall Street Journal*, Beattie had this to say about the ad business:

Trevor Beattie

"I love the industry, but I hate the people. I think they're all jerks. They're shallow, insecure, arrogant, jealous, bitter, unforgiving, small-minded: a group of cheapskates and thieves."

Torakusu Yamaha built Japan's first organ in 1885. To find out whether it would pass muster, he and a friend carried it on a pole 159 miles to Tokyo.

Ah, Those Golden Years

CEOs who reach 65 and retire do not have to worry about where their next meal is coming from. The *New York Times*, with the help of the Corporate Library, figured out the pension arrangements for the following 20 CEOs.

CHIEF EXECUTIVE	COMPANY	ANNUAL RETIREMENT BENEFIT
Henry A. McKinnell Jr.	Pfizer	$6.5 million
Lee R. Raymond	ExxonMobil	$5.9 million
Edward E. Whitacre Jr.	SBC	$5.5 million
William W. McGuire	UnitedHealth Group	$5.1 million
Robert L. Nardelli	Home Depot	$3.9 million
Reuben Mark	Colgate-Palmolive	$3.7 million
Kenneth D. Lewis	Bank of America	$3.6 million
Samuel J. Palmisano	IBM	$3.4 million
Jeffrey R. Immelt	General Electric	$2.9 million
James J. Mulva	ConocoPhillips	$2.7 million
Richard K. Davidson	Union Pacific	$2.7 million
Arthur F. Ryan	Prudential	$2.6 million
Harold M. Messmer Jr.	Robert Half	$2.6 million
Nolan D. Archibald	Black & Decker	$2.6 million
Robert A. Eckert	Mattel	$2.5 million
Patrick T. Stokes	Anheuser-Busch	$2.5 million
Lewis Hay III	FPL Group	$2.4 million
Sidney Taurel	Eli Lilly	$2.3 million
E. Neville Isdell	Coca-Cola	$2.3 million
Douglas H. McCorkindale	Gannett	$2.2 million

TOP 10

Donors to K–12 Education

1. Bill & Melinda Gates Foundation	$246 million
2. Walton Family Foundation	$77 million
3. Annenberg Foundation	$40 million
4. Carnegie Corp. of New York	$25 million
5. Lilly Endowment	$23 million
6. New York Community Trust	$21 million
7. Ford Foundation	$20 million
8. W. K. Kellogg Foundation	$20 million
9. William & Flora Hewlett Foundation	$19 million
10. Oberkotter Foundation	$18 million

Coffee ranks second in value only to oil as a world commodity. The heaviest coffee drinkers are the Scandinavians. Finland tops the league standings, followed by Sweden, Norway, and Denmark. An adult in Finland will typically down four or five cups of coffee a day. The United States consumes one-third of the coffee produced in the world, but it ranks sixteenth in per capita consumption. The biggest jump in consumption in recent years has come in Japan, which came from nowhere to number three in the world in coffee intake.

Texas-based computer maker Dell has 10,000 employees in India, nearly 20 percent of its entire workforce. Dell operations in India include three call centers, a product testing laboratory, and a software development unit.

It Pays to Remember H&R Block

KEN JENNINGS, a soft-spoken software engineer from Salt Lake City, Utah, broke all the records on the quiz show *Jeopardy!* when he won $2.5 million after 74 appearances in 2004. His reign ended when he gave an incorrect question to this answer:

Ken Jennings

"Most of this firm's 70,000 seasonal employees work only four months a year."

Jennings guessed: "What is FedEx?"

The correct question was: "What is H&R Block?"

H&R Block, based in Kansas City, is a tax preparation firm that operates more than 10,000 offices throughout the United States. The only company with more outlets—nearly 14,000—is McDonald's. H&R Block outposts do the tax returns for 16 million Americans.

Jennings said that since he does his own returns, he never encountered an H&R Block office. But he won't be doing his own tax returns anymore: H&R Block offered him free financial services for life so that he "would never forget their name again."

World's Largest Magazine Publishers

Advance Publications

Conde Nast Publications: *Allure*, *Architectural Digest*, *Bon Appetit*, *Conde Nast House & Garden*, *Conde Nast Traveler*, *Glamour*, *Gourmet*, *GQ*, *Lucky*, *The New Yorker*, *Parade Publications*, *Parade*, *React*, *Self*, *Tatler*, *Vanity Fair*, *Vogue*, *Wired*, *The World of Interiors* **Fairchild:** *Beauty Biz*, *Beauty Report International* (published in English and French), *Brand Marketing*, *Bride's*, *Children's Business*, *Daily News Record*, *Details*, *Elegant Bride*, *Executive Technology*, *Footwear News*, *German*, *High Points*, *Home Furnishings News*, *InFurniture*, *Jane*, *Modern Brides*, *Salon News*, *Supermarket News*, *Vitals*, *W*, *Women's Wear Daily* **Other:** *Golf Digest*, *Golf for Women*, *Golf World*, *Golf World Business*

Hachette Filipacchi (subsidiary of Lagardère)

North America: *American Photo*, *Boating*, *Car and Driver*, *Car Stereo Review's Mobile Entertainment*, *Cycle World*, *ELLE*, *Elle Decor*, *ELLEgirl*, *Flying*, *Home*, *Metropolitan Home*, *Popular Photography*, *Premiere*, *Road & Track*, *Showboats International*, *Sound & Vision*, *Travel Holiday*, *Woman's Day*, *Woman's Day Special Interest Publications* **France:** *Action Auto Moto*, *Automobiles Classiques*, *Bambi*, *Bon Voyage*, *Choc*, *Corse-Matin*, *ELLE*, *ELLE A TABLE*, *ELLE DECORATION*, *Entrevue*, *Femina Hebdo*, *France Dimanche*, *ICI Paris*, *ISA*, *Jeune & Jolie*, *Joypad*, *Joystick*, *La Corse Votre Hebdo*, *La Provence*, *Le Journal de Mickey*, *Le Journal du Dimanche*, *L'echo des Savanes*, *Maximal*, *Mickey Jeux*, *Mickey Parade*, *Minnie Mag*, *Nice-Matin*, *OK!*, *Podium*, *Onze Mondial*, *Parents*, *Paris Match*, *Pariscope*, *Photo*, *Picsou Magazine*, *Playstation 2*, *Premiere*, *P'tit Loup*, *Super Picsou Géant*, *Tele 7 Jeux*, *Tele*

7 Jours, *Telecable Satellite Hebdo*, *Top Famille Magazine*, *TV Hebdo*, *Var-Matin*, *Week-End*, *Winnie*, *Winnie Jeux*, *Winnie Lecture*

Hearst Corporation

Cosmopolitan, *COSMO!*, *Country Living*, *Country Living Gardener*, *Esquire*, *Good Housekeeping*, *Harper's BAZAAR*, *House Beautiful*, *Marie Claire*, *O, The Oprah Magazine*, *Popular Mechanics*, *Redbook*, *Seventeen*, *SHOP Etc.*, *SmartMoney*, *Town & Country*, *Town & Country TRAVEL*, *Veranda* **National Magazine Company, UK:** *Best*, *Coast*, *Company*, *CosmoGIRL!*, *Cosmopolitan*, *Cosmopolitan Bride*, *Cosmopolitan Hair and Beauty*, *Country Living*, *Esquire*, *Good Housekeeping*, *Good Housekeeping Institute*, *Harpers & Queen*, *House Beautiful*, *Men's Health*, *Prima*, *Prima Baby*, *Reveal*, *Runner's World*, *She*, *You & Your Wedding*, *Zest* **Hearst Magazines International:** Publishes 141 editions in 32 languages and distributes in more than 100 countries. Titles include *Cosmopolitan*, *CosmoGIRL!*, *Country Living*, *Good Housekeeping*, *House Beautiful*, *Redbook*, *Popular Mechanics*, *Esquire*, and more.

Primedia

Automobile: *4Wheel & Off-Road*, *4Wheel Drive & Sport Utility*, *5.0 Mustang & Super Fords*, *ATV Rider*, *Car Audio and Electronics*, *Car Craft*, *Chevy High Performance*, *Circle Track*, *Classic Trucks*, *Corvette Fever*, *Custom Classic Trucks*, *Custom Rodder*, *Diesel Power*, *Dirt Rider*, *European Car*, *Eurotuner*, *Four Wheeler*, *GM High-Tech Performance*, *High Performance Pontiac*, *Honda Tuning*, *Hot Bike*, *Hot Rod*, *Hot Rod Bikes*, *Import Tuner*, *Jp*, *Kit Car*, *Lowrider*, *Lowrider Arte*, *Mini Truckin'*, *Mopar Muscle*, *Motor Trend*, *Motorcycle Cruiser*, *Motorcyclist*, *Muscle Mustangs & Fast Fords*, *Mustang & Fords*, *Mustang Monthly*, *Off-Road*, *Popular Hot Rodding*, *Rod & Custom*, *Sport Compact Car*, *Sport Rider*, *Sport Truck*, *Stock Car Racing*, *Street Chopper*, *Street Rodder*, *Super Chevy*, *Super Street*, *Truck Trend*, *Truckin'*, *Turbo & High-Tech*

(Continued on page 30)

(Continued from page 29)

Performance, *Vette* **Action Sports:** *Bike*, *Canoe & Kayak*, *Climbing*, *Powder*, *SG*, *Skateboarder*, *Slam*, *Snowboarder*, *Surfer*, *Surfing* **Crafts:** *CrafTrends*, *Creative Machine Embroidery*, *Creating Keepsakes*, *McCall's Quilting*, *McCall's Quick Quilts*, *Paper Crafts*, *Quilter's Newsletter*, *Quiltmaker*, *Sew News*, *Simple Scrapbooks*, *Step by Step Beads* **Equestrian:** *Dressage Today*, *EQUUS*, *Horse & Rider*, *Practical Horseman* **Gems:** *Colored Stone*, *Lapidary Journal* **Marine:** *Boatworks*, *Power & Motoryacht*, *SAIL*, *Voyaging* **Entertainment:** *Home Technology & Photography*, *Home Theater*, *Petersen's PHOTOgraphic*, *Shutterbug*, *Soap Opera Digest*, *Soap Opera Weekly*, *Stereophile* **History:** *American History*, *America's Civil War*, *Aviation History*, *British Heritage*, *Civil War Times*, *Military History*, *Quarterly Journal of Military History*, *Vietnam*, *Wild West*, *World War II* **Outdoors:** *Bowhunter*, *Florida Sportsman*, *Fly Fisherman*, *Game & Fish*, *Gun Dog*, *Guns & Ammo*, *Handguns*, *In-Fisherman*, *In-Fisherman Bass Guide*, *In-Fisherman Catfish Guide*, *In-Fisherman Ice Fishing Guide*, *In-Fisherman Walleye Guide*, *North American Whitetail*, *Petersen's Bowhunting*, *Petersen's Hunting*, *Rifle Shooter*, *Shooting Times*, *Shotgun News*, *Walleye In-Sider*, *Wildfowl* **Agriculture:** *Apply*, *BEEF*, *Corn & Soybean Digest*, *Delta Farm Press*, *Farm Industry News*, *Hay & Forage Grower*, *National Hog Farmer*, *Southeast Farm Press*, *Southwest Farm Press*, *Western Farm Press* **Construction:** *Cement Americas*, *Concrete Products* **Electrical:** *Electrical Construction & Maintenance*, *Electrical Marketing*, *Electrical Wholesaling* **Electronics:** *Power Electronics Technology*, *RF Design* **Entertainment Technology:** *Broadcast Engineering*, *Electronic Musician*, *Entertainment Design*, *Lighting Dimensions*, *millimeter*, *MIX*, *Radio magazine*, *Remix*, *Sound & Video Contractor*, *Staging Rental Operations*, *Video Systems* **Financial Services:** *Registered Rep.*, *Trusts & Estates* **Government & Public Services:** *American City & County*, *American School & University*, *Grounds Maintenance*, *Rental Equipment Register* **Health Services:** *Fitness Business Pro*, *Homecare* **Marketing:** *Catalog Age*, *DIRECT*, *Operations & Fulfillment*, *PROMO* **Meeting and Event Planning:**

Association Meetings, *Corporate Meetings & Incentives*, *Insurance Conference Planner*, *Medical Meetings*, *Religious Conference Manager*, *Special Events* **Mining:** *Mine & Quarry Trader*, *Rock Products* **Mobile Communications:** *Mobile Radio Technology* **Power:** *Transmission & Distribution World* **Printing/Converting:** *American Printer*, *Paper Film & Foil Converter* **Real Estate:** *National Real Estate Investor*, *Retail Traffic* **Security:** *Access Control & Security Systems* **Telecommunications:** *Telephony*, *Wireless Review* **Textiles:** *Modern Uniforms*, *Profitable Embroiderer*, *Stitches*, *Wearables Business* **Transportation:** *American Trucker*, *Fire Chief*, *Fleet Owner*, *Modern Bulk Transporter*, *Refrigerated Transporter*, *Trailer & Body Builders*, *Ward's AutoWorld*, *Ward's Dealer Business* **Waste and Environment:** *Waste Age*

Time Warner

25 Beautiful Gardens, *25 Beautiful Homes*, *25 Beautiful Kitchens*, *4x4*, *Aeroplane*, *All You*, *Amateur Gardening*, *Amateur Photographer*, *Ambientes*, *Angler's Mail*, *Audi Magazine*, *BabyTalk*, *Balance*, *Bird Keeper*, *Bulfinch Press*, *Business 2.0*, *Cage & Aviary Birds*, *Caravan*, *Center Street*, *Chat*, *Chilango*, *Classic Boat*, *Coastal Living*, *Cooking Light*, *Cottage Living*, *Country Homes & Interiors*, *Country Life*, *Cycle Sport*, *Cycling Weekly*, *Decanter*, *Elle*, *Entertainment Weekly*, *Essence*, *Essentials*, *European Boat Builder*, *Eventing*, *EXP*, *Expansión*, *Family Circle* (UK), *Field & Stream*, *Fortune*, *Fortune Asia*, *Fortune Europe*, *FSB: Fortune Small Business*, *Golf Magazine*, *Golf Monthly*, *Guitar*, *Hair*, *Health*, *Hi-Fi News*, *Homes & Gardens*, *Horse*, *Horse & Hound*, *Ideal Home*, *In Style*, *In Style* (UK), *International Boat Industry*, *Land Rover World*, *Life*, *Livingetc*, *Loaded*, *Loaded Fashion*, *Manufactura*, *Marie Claire* (UK), *MBR (Mountain Bike Rider)*, *MiniWorld*, *Mizz*, *Model Collector*, *Money*, *Motor Boat & Yachting*, *Motor Boats Monthly*, *Motor Caravan*, *MotorBoating*, *Navigator**, *NME*, *Now*, *Nuts*, *Obras*, *Outdoor Life*, *Parenting*, *Park Home & Holiday Caravan*, *People*, *People en Español*, *Pick Me Up*, *Popular Science*, *Practical Boat Owner*, *Practical*

(Continued on page 32)

(Continued from page 31)

Parenting, *Prediction*, *Progressive Farmer*, *Quién*, *Quo*, *Racecar Engineering*, *Real Simple*, *Ride BMX*, *Rugby World*, *Salt Water Sportsman*, *Ships Monthly*, *Shoot Monthly*, *Shooting Times*, *Ski*, *Skiing*, *Soaplife*, *Southern Accents*, *Southern Living*, *Sporting Gun*, *Sports Illustrated*, *Sports Illustrated For Kids*, *Stamp Magazine*, *Sunset*, *SuperBike*, *Targeted Media Inc.*, *Teen People*, *The Field*, *The Golf*, *The Golf+*, *The Railway Magazine*, *The Shooting Gazette*, *This Old House*, *This Old House Ventures*, *Time*, *Time Asia*, *Time Atlantic*, *Time Australia*, *Time Canada*, *Time For Kids*, *TransWorld Business*, *TransWorld Motocross*, *TransWorld Skateboarding*, *TransWorld Snowboarding*, *TransWorld Surf*, *TV & Satellite Week*, *TV Easy*, *TVTimes*, *Uncut*, *VolksWorld*, *Vuelo*, *Wallpaper**, *Warner Books*, *Warner Faith*, *Web User*, *Wedding*, *What Camera*, *What Digital Camera*, *What's on TV*, *Who*, *Woman*, *Woman & Home*, *Woman's Own*, *Woman's Weekly*, *Women & Golf*, *World Soccer*, *Yachting*, *Yachting Monthly*, *Yachting World*, *Yachts* **American Express Publishing Corporation (partial ownership/management):** *Departures*, *Food & Wine*, *SkyGuide*, *Travel & Leisure*, *Your Company* **Magazines listed under Warner Brothers:** *DC Comics*, *Mad Magazine*, *Milestone*, *Paradox*, *Vertigo*

Whole Foods Market, the Austin, Texas, based chain of natural foods supermarkets, has a salary cap policy that limits the cash compensation paid to any officer to 14 times the average salary of full-time employees. The average salary in 2004 was $30,500, which meant top executives could make no more than $427,000 in cash compensation. CEO John Mackey made $368,000 in 2004.

John Mackey

Average Paychecks of Workers in New York City in 2004

CEO	$177,170
Surgeon	$165,640
Internist	$161,330
Obstetrician/gynecologist	$156,850
Salesperson at a financial services company	$146,140
Construction manager	$73,330
Registered nurse	$68,450
Dental hygienist	$64,690
Editor	$61,700
Real estate broker	$60,580
Full-time actor	$57,190*
Writer/author	$56,760
Reporter	$55,140
Massage therapist	$53,120
Fitness trainer	$51,300
Preschool teacher	$46,750
Chef	$45,760
Substance abuse counselor	$39,770
Bartender	$23,360
Retail sales clerk	$23,030
Home health aide	$18,400
Cashier	$16,970
Manicurist/pedicurist	$16,430
Shampooer	$16,030
Service station attendant	$15,370
Fast-food cook	$15,320

**2003 figure*

Progress of Women in Corporate Board Rooms

Seats held by women on boards of directors of Fortune 500 companies:

1995: 9.6%
2003: 13.6%

At this rate of change, women will still hold less than 25 percent of board seats by 2025.

A study by Catalyst, a New York nonprofit group, shows that in 2003, 54 of the Fortune 500 companies had no women on their boards.

IN A CLASS BY ITSELF: Golden West Financial, based in Oakland, California, is a savings and lending institution. Of its nine directors, five are women.

France leads the world in annual wine consumption, at 15.8 gallons (60 l) per person; Italy follows at 14.3 gallons (54 l) per person. In the United States, per capita consumption is 2 gallons (7.6 l) a year, though Americans consume 19 percent of the wine produced in the world.

Guinness Is Good for You

GUINNESS, virtually the official drink of Ireland, is made from barley, water, hops, and yeast—and it's sold around the world to the tune of ten million glasses every day. The beer was first brewed in Dublin in 1759 by Arthur Guinness, whose signature still graces every bottle and can of Guinness. The company moved its headquarters from Dublin to London in 1886, but the family continued to control the company for another 100 years. A series of mergers in the 1980s and 1990s brought the brand into the cellar of Diageo, the world's largest alcoholic beverage company.

Guinness is almost as well known for its advertising—"Guinness Is Good for You"—as for its distinctive flavor. It first began advertising in 1929 under the aegis of the British ad agency S. H. Benson (where Dorothy Sayers worked as a copywriter). In 1955, as a way to settle arguments in pubs, the company began publishing what became the bestselling copyrighted English language book of all time, *Guinness World Records*. In 2001, the company sold the title for $85 million to British toy company Gullane (creators of Sooty and Thomas the Tank Engine).

According to the Fortune 500 list, only 205 corporations recorded revenues of more than $10.8 billion in 2004. However, one company, Pfizer, the world's largest pharmaceutical manufacturer, had revenues of more than $10.8 billion from just one product, its cholesterol-lowering drug Lipitor.

PROFILE

Deere & Company

IT'S DIFFICULT TO FIND ANYONE who has something bad to say about John Deere. Not the 46,000 employees, who enjoy good pay and benefits, including an outstanding health plan; not the United Auto Workers, which represents the hourly factory workers; not the 400,000 residents of the Quad Cities area straddling the Iowa-Illinois border, where Deere is the largest employer; not the 1,400 dealers who sell John Deere lawn mowers, utility vehicles, tractors, combines, harvesters, and other agricultural equipment.

A strong vein of integrity runs through this American company, which was founded in 1837 by John Deere, a blacksmith from Vermont who moved to the frontier town of Grand Detour, Illinois, in 1836. There he invented the first self-cleaning plow. "Integrity means telling the truth, keeping our word, and treating others with fairness and respect," states a Deere document spelling out the company's values. In an age of rampant corporate corruption, Deere has stayed its course—the company has remained untouched by scandal throughout its nearly 170-year history.

John Deere

The company's resolve has been proven during hard times. In 1931, three employees of the People's Savings Bank in Moline, Illinois, were found to have embezzled $1.2 million. Thousands of Deere employees had their savings accounts at this bank, which was in danger of going under. The company stepped in to write a check for $1.2 million to keep the bank afloat, securing all the deposits. During the Depression many farmers found it difficult to make payments on the loans they had taken to buy Deere equipment.

The company decided to carry the debt on their books for years without demanding immediate payments.

Over the first 168 years of its existence, Deere had only eight chief executives, all of whom were family members, until Robert A. Hanson took the helm in 1982. In 1955, William Hewitt, a member of the Deere clan through marriage, took over the company and became instrumental in its emergence as a modern corporation with a global presence. One of his first actions after moving to the headquarters in Moline was to commission architect Eero Saarinen to design a spectacular, seven-story, steel-and-glass headquarters building placed in the middle of a ravine; it was one of the last structures designed by Saarinen before his death in 1961.

Fortune writer Charles Burck described how Hewitt moved Deere into the international arena. He called in Harry Pence, one of Deere's top factory managers, and asked him to investigate possible acquisitions overseas. Pence said: "Hell, Bill, I don't even know where these places are." Hewitt responded: "Harry, go and buy you and your wife plane tickets, fly around the world, and find out where they are." Pence went off on a two-month trip, leading to the acquisition of a German tractor company, Lanz, and the start of Deere plants in five other countries.

Hundreds of thousands of visitors visit Moline every year to see the John Deere Pavilion and the John Deere Collectors Center. On display there are products, new and old, from John Deere's history, including a replica of the one that started it all, the self-cleaning plow.

CONNECTICUT IS HOME TO MANY FIRSTS: HAMBURGER (1895), POLAROID CAMERA (1934), HELICOPTER (1939), COLOR TELEVISION SET (1948), AND NUCLEAR-POWERED SUBMARINE (1954).

FRATRICIDE

The Hafts

HERBERT H. HAFT was a pharmacist who, starting from a single store in the Adams Morgan section of Washington, D.C., built a discount drugstore chain, Dart Drug; a discount auto parts chain, Trak Auto; and a discount bookstore chain, Crown Books. He then became a successful greenmailer, accumulating stock in different companies (Jack Eckerd, Federated Department Stores, Safeway Stores, and Stop & Shop) by threatening a takeover and settling for a payout considerably above the price he had paid for the shares.

Haft's wife and children worked in the business, but in 1993 the family came to blows. Herbert fired his eldest son, Robert, and drove his wife, Gloria, and his daughter, Linda, out of the business. His 46-year marriage collapsed. Haft's younger son, Ronald, took his father's side in the dispute, but after a year he also clashed with his father, who sued him.

In 1994, after his divorce, Herbert met Myrna Ruben, who became his companion. In the summer of 2004, Haft was admitted to Sibley Hospital in Washington, suffering from liver and kidney failure. His son Robert picked that time to sue his father, claiming he was owed $2 million. Haft's daughter, hearing that her father planned to marry Ruben, went to court trying to block the marriage, declaring that her father was mentally incompetent to make such a decision. A court-appointed psychiatrist found that Haft was competent.

Haft amended his will to make it clear that he was not leaving anything to his three children. On August 18, 2004, while he was in the intensive care unit, he married Ruben. On August 23, he turned 84. On September 1, he died. Haft had been in and out of the courts for years, so much so that writer Walter Kirin said he dissipated most of his fortune, once valued at close to $1 billion—his final estate had assets totaling $50 million.

Who Has the Most Retail Nameplates Around the World?

1. **McDonald's** 31,500
2. **7-Eleven** 27,900
3. **Burger King** 11,200
4. **KFC** 11,100
5. **Citicorp** 11,000
6. **H&R Block** 11,000
7. **Pizza Hut** 10,600
8. **Edward Jones** more than 9,000
9. **Starbucks** more than 9,000
10. **Radio Shack** about 7,000
11. **Taco Bell** 6,800
12. **Wendy's** 6,700
13. **Wells Fargo** 6,100

Who Reads Newspapers Anymore?

The circulation of newspapers has been declining steadily over the past ten years. In the six-month period ending in March 2005, 814 daily papers suffered a 1.9 percent drop in daily circulation, and 643 newspapers suffered a 2.5 percent drop on Sundays, from the same period the year before. The decline represented the biggest erosion of readership in more than a decade.

What's in a Name?

TESCO, the largest supermarket operator in Britain, was named after the initials of its leading supplier, T. E. Stockwell, and the first two letters of founder Jack Cohen's last name.

WAITROSE, an upscale British grocer, was named for the company's founders, Wallace Waite and Arthur Rose.

ASDA, the Wal-Mart-owned discount store operator in Britain, took its name from its beginning as Associated Dairies.

KODAK is a name invented by the company's founder, George Eastman, whose favorite letter was "K." "It seems a strong, incisive sort of letter," he said.

IKEA is a combination of the initials of its founder, Ingvar Kamprad, and the first letter of a family farm, Elmtaryd, located near the Swedish town of Agunnaryd.

FIG NEWTON cookies are named after the town of Newton outside of Boston. The official history of Nabisco, *Out of the Cracker Barrel*, by William Cahn, cites the company practice of naming cookies and crackers after towns near Boston. In addition to Fig Newtons, there were cookies and crackers named for Brighton, Boston, Cambridge (salts), Beacon Hill, Shrewsbury, and Melrose.

LEVI'S jeans were named for the founder, Levi Strauss.

Britain's apparel chain **FCUK** stands for French Connection United Kingdom.

ADOLF HITLER'S FAVORITE CAR, THE MERCEDES, WAS NAMED FOR THE GRANDDAUGHTER OF A RABBI.

TOP 10

U.S. Philanthropists*

1. Gordon and Betty Moore	Intel cofounder	$7.0 billion
2. Bill and Melinda Gates	Microsoft cofounder	$5.4 billion
3. Warren Buffett	Investor	$2.6 billion
4. George Soros	Investor	$2.3 billion
5. Eli and Edythe Broad	SunAmerica, KB Home founder	$1.4 billion
6. James and Virginia Stowers	American Century Investments founder	$1.2 billion
7. Walton family	Family of Wal-Mart founder	$1.1 billion
8. Alfred Mann	Medical devices	$933 million
9. Michael and Susan Dell	Dell founder	$933 million
10. George Kaiser	Oil, gas, banking, real estate	$617 million

**Money pledged or given, 2001–2005*

5 European Stocks You Should Have Bought in 1985

East Surrey Holdings (ESH), based in Surrey, England, is a British company that supplies drinking water to towns in the south of England and natural gas to the greater Belfast area.

€1,000 invested in East Surrey shares at the start of 1985 would have turned into €346,472 if held through March 31, 2005.

Homeserve (HSV), based in the town of Walsall, England, sells insurance policies to private homes.

€1,000 invested in Homeserve at the end of 1984 would have escalated to €312,641 by March 31, 2005.

Barcelona-based **Gas Natural SDG** (CTG) is a gas and electricity supplier in Spain. It also distributes gas in Argentina, Brazil, Colombia, Mexico, Puerto Rico, and Italy.

€1,000 invested in CTG shares at the start of 1985 would have jumped in value to €179,269 by March 31, 2005.

Dublin-based **Anglo Irish Bank Corp.** (AGBKY) is a leading lender to businesses. In terms of market value, it ranks seventh among stocks listed on the Irish Stock Exchange.

€1,000 invested in Anglo Irish at the end of 1984 would have been worth €112,251 on March 31, 2005.

Autostrada Torino-Milano (AT) operates the toll road that runs from Milan to Turin in Italy.

€1,000 invested in AT at the start of 1985 would have increased in value to €91,628 by March 31, 2005.

5 European Stocks You Should Have Avoided in 1985

Bremer Vulkan Verbund (BVU), based in Bremen, Germany, is a shipbuilder and machine tool manufacturer.

€1,000 invested in Bremer Vulkan shares at the end of 1984 would have dropped in value to €4.68 by March 31, 2005.

Water Hall Group (WTH) operates landfills and quarries in the United Kingdom.

€1,000 invested in Water Hall stock at the end of 1984 would have declined to €19.14 by March 31, 2005.

PlanIT Holdings (PLN) is a British company that develops software for the woodworking, engineering, and automotive industries.

€1,000 invested in PlanIT shares at the start of 1985 would have eroded to €24.60 by March 31, 2005.

London-based **Ultrasis** (ULT) develops therapeutic services to help customers deal with chronic conditions such as insomnia, depression, stress, and irritable bowel syndrome. Brand names include Beating the Blues, Drink & Drug Wise, and Calm Workplace.

€1,000 invested in Ultrasis at the end of 1984 would have plunged to €28.10 by March 31, 2005.

Dublin-based **Aminex** (AEXL) develops oil and gas reserves in Russia, the United States, Africa, Asia, and Europe.

€1,000 invested in Aminex shares at the start of 1985 would have declined to €29.99 by March 31, 2005.

Note: Final return assumes that all dividends and distributions were reinvested in stock.

The 100 Best Companies to Work for in America

The first survey of the best companies to work for appeared in 1984 in a book titled *The 100 Best Companies to Work for in America*. Written by Robert Levering and Milton Moskowitz, the author of this compilation, it zoomed onto the bestseller lists shortly after its publication. The following were the companies on that initial list:

3M
A.G. Edwards
Advanced Micro Devices
Analog Devices
Anheuser-Busch
Apple Computer
Armstrong World
Atlantic Richfield
Baxter Travenol
Bell Laboratories
Borg-Warner
Celestial Seasonings
Citicorp
Control Data
CRS Sirrine
Cummins Engine
Dana
Dayton Hudson
Deere & Company
Delta Airlines
Digital Equipment
Donnelly Mirrors
Doyle Dane Bernbach
DuPont
Eastman Kodak
Electro Scientific
Erie Insurance
Exxon
Fisher-Price Toys
General Electric
General Mills
Goldman Sachs
H.B. Fuller
H.J. Heinz
Hallmark Cards
Herman Miller
Hewitt Associates
Hewlett-Packard

IBM
Inland Steel
Intel
Johnson & Johnson
JC Penney
JPMorgan
Knight-Ridder
Kollmorgen
Leo Burnett
Levi Strauss
Liebert Corporation
Linnton Plywood
Los Angeles Dodgers
Lowe's
Marion Labs
Mary Kay
Maytag
McCormick
Merle Norman
Moog
Nissan
Nordstrom
Northrop Corporation
Northwestern Mutual Life
Nucor
Odetics
Olga
People Express Airlines
Physio-Control
Pitney Bowes
Polaroid
Preston Trucking
Procter & Gamble
Publix Super Markets
Quad/Graphic
Rainier Bancorporation
Random House
Raychem
Reader's Digest
REI
Remington Products
ROLM
Ryder
Saga
SC Johnson
Security Pacific
Shell Oil
Southern California Edison
Springs Industries
Steelcase
Tandem Computers
Tandy
Tektronix
Tenneco
Time Inc.
Trammell Crow
Viking Freight
Wal-Mart
Westin Hotels
Weyerhaeuser
W.L. Gore
Worthington Industries

The 100 Best Companies to Work for in America, 1993

A completely revised edition of the book, still called *The 100 Best Companies to Work for in America*, was published in 1993. Only 55 of the companies on the 1985 list survived. The 45 new companies were:

Alagasco
American Cast Iron Pipe
Apogee Enterprises
Avis
Baptist Hospital of Miami
BE&K
Ben & Jerry's
Beth Israel Hospital (Boston)
Chaparral Steel
Compaq Computer
Cooper Tire
Corning
Cray Research
Fel-Pro
First Federal Bank of California
Great Plains Software
Haworth
Hershey
Honda of America
J.M. Smucker
Kellogg
Lands' End
Lincoln Electric
Lotus Development
Lyondell Petrochemical
Marquette Electronics
Merck
Methodist Hospital (Houston)
Microsoft
Morrison & Foerster
Motorola
Patagonia
Rosenbluth International
SAS Institute
Southwest Airlines
Springfield ReManufacturing
Syntex
TDIndustries
Tennant
UNUM
USAA
U.S. West
Valassis
Wegmans
Xerox

The 100 Best Companies to Work For, 1998–2005

In 1998, the list, now called "The 100 Best Companies to Work For," began appearing annually in *Fortune* magazine. The Great Place to Work Institute of San Francisco introduced a new methodology, the heart of which is a survey instrument, the Trust Index, that is answered by 350 randomly selected employees at each candidate company. This enabled Levering and Moskowitz to rank the companies for the first time. During the first eight years of the *Fortune* run, only 22 companies made the list every single year. They were:

A.G. Edwards
American Cast Iron Pipe
Cisco Systems
FedEx
First Horizon
Four Seasons
Goldman Sachs
J.M. Smucker
Marriott
MBNA
Microsoft
Nordstrom
Publix
REI
SAS Institute
Synovus
TDIndustries
Timberland
Valassis
W.L. Gore
Wegmans
Whole Foods Market

Companies on the original list in 1984 that appear on the list in 2005:

General Mills
Goldman Sachs
W.L. Gore
SC Johnson
Nordstrom
Procter & Gamble

10 Best Workplaces in the United Kingdom, 2005

	BUSINESS
1. ?Whatif!	Consultants
2. Bain & Co.	Consultants
3. Data Connection	Software
4. United Welsh Housing	Social services and government agencies
5. Asthma UK	Charity
6. Beaverbrooks	Retail jeweler
7. Procter & Gamble UK	Consumer goods
8. W.L. Gore	Products like Gore-Tex
9. Frontier Economics	Professional services
10. Microsoft	Software

The New York Yankees have the highest payroll in organized baseball:

$208,306,817

The Tampa Bay Devil Rays have the lowest payroll in organized baseball:

$29,679,067

ERGO: Yankee star Alex Rodriguez almost makes as much as the entire Devil Rays roster.

EVERY YEAR DENNY'S RESTAURANTS SERVE 140 MILLION EGGS AND 130 MILLION PANCAKES.

Where Do MBAs from Top Business Schools Go to Work?

Graduates of the Stanford Business School, class of 2004, took jobs in the following fields after their graduation:

SERVICE SECTOR	PERCENT OF CLASS	MEDIAN TOTAL PAY
Management consulting	18	$140,000
E-commerce/Internet	8	$125,500
Private equity	8	$230,000
Investment banking/brokerage	6	$142,500
Hedge funds	5	$197,500
Investment management	5	$136,375
Entertainment/media	4	$131,250
Financial services/diversified	4	$140,000
Nonprofit/government	4	$93,200
Real estate	4	$135,000
Venture capital	4	$168,500
Consumer services	3	$125,000
Health/human services	2	$134,000
Other	4	$121,000

MANUFACTURING SECTOR	PERCENT OF CLASS	MEDIAN TOTAL PAY
Consumer products	6	$108,200
Biotech/pharm/medical	4	$129,252
Computers (software)	4	$132,250
Computers (hardware)	2	$276,500
Networking/telecom	2	$117,000
Other	3	$129,252

10 Largest Employers* in New York City

	EMPLOYEES
1. New York Presbyterian Hospital/Columbia University Medical Center/Weill Cornell Medical Center	30,000
2. Citigroup	24,800
3. JPMorgan Chase	23,400
4. Verizon	18,600
5. Continuum Health Partners (Beth Israel, St. Luke's, Roosevelt Hospitals, Long Island College Hospital, New York Eye & Ear Infirmary)	16,800
6. New York University	13,200
7. North Shore–Long Island Jewish Health System	12,700
8. Columbia University	12,500
9. Federated Department Stores (Macy's, Bloomingdale's)	12,200
10. St. Vincent Catholic Medical Centers (Catholic Medical Centers of Brooklyn and Queens, Saint Vincent Hospital and Medical Center of New York, and Sisters of Charity Healthcare on Staten Island)	11,900

**2004 totals, excluding government agencies*

10 Largest Employers* in Douglas County, Kansas

	EMPLOYEES
1. University of Kansas	9,555
2. Lawrence Public Schools	1,687
3. Pearson Government Solutions	1,540
4. City of Lawrence	1,397
5. Lawrence Memorial Hospital	1,160
6. Hallmark Cards	787
7. Baker University	623
8. The World Company (operates a daily paper and Sunflower cable/telephone company)	584
9. Berry Plastics	500
10. K-mart Distribution Center	492

**2005 totals, according to the Lawrence, Kansas, Chamber of Commerce*

HANNIBAL, LEADING HIS CARTHAGINIAN TROOPS IN AN ASSAULT ON ROME IN 218 B.C., STOPPED AT THE TOWN OF VERGÈZE IN THE SOUTH OF FRANCE AND QUAFFED FROM AN UNDERGROUND SPRING THE WATER KNOWN AROUND THE WORLD TODAY AS PERRIER.

PROFILE

Cadbury-Schweppes

HERE'S A COMPANY steeped in British history that is now so global that more than 80 percent of sales come from outside its home country—especially from the United States. There are two main lines of descent.

The Schweppes business dates from 1783. The name comes from Jacob Schweppe, a German-born Swiss who concocted a mineral water sold under claims that it was good for your health.

The Cadbury business was started by a young Quaker, John Cadbury, in 1824. Cadbury added massive amounts of sugar to naturally bitter cocoa to produce the sweet chocolate bars that have destroyed the teeth of many generations in Britain.

L. Rose & Co., a firm acquired by Schweppes in 1957, has a lineage of its own that goes back to 1867, when all British ships were required by law to carry lime juice to ward off scurvy. (It was this practice that resulted in the appellation "Limey" for Britons.) Rose was the supplier of that juice, which is still part of Schweppes's fruit juice line.

Cadbury got together with Schweppes in 1969. Ever since, streams of companies enter and leave the fold. Among the brands once acquired and then discarded are Mounds, Almond Joy, Typhoo Tea, Hartley Jams, and Chivers Marmalade. At one point, in their home country, they were distributing wines, bleaches, and household disinfectants (the Jeyes line), household cleansers (Scrubbs Ammonia), and fire-lighters (Wonderflame).

Cadbury-Schweppes has established a formidable presence in the U.S. market by dint of acquisition after acquisition. In their American larder are: Snapple, 7-UP, Mott's, Dr Pepper, Canada Dry, Welch's soda, Sunkist soda, Nantucket Nectars, Certs, Chiclets, Hawaiian Punch, A&W Root Beer, Hires Root Beer, Halls Cough

Drops, Certs, Dentyne, and the Bubbas bubble gums (Hubba Bubba, Bubblicious). That makes them the third-largest soft drink purveyor, after Coca-Cola and Pepsi-Cola. And they're proud to tell us that they are now selling 100,000 tons of Halls every year.

Rewards of Smoking

Tobacco companies have been under fire from health authorities for more than 35 years. At the start of 1970, Philip Morris stock was selling for $35 a share. Assume an investor bought 100 shares then for an outlay of $3,500. Flash forward to March 31, 2005, by which time Philip Morris had changed its corporate name to Altria. If the investor had kept the initial holding, neither adding nor subtracting from it, stock splits would have turned those 100 shares into 4,800 shares worth $313,872. And along the way the investor would have collected cash dividends totaling $126,902.

Meanwhile, over those 35 years, an estimated 3.9 million Americans died of lung cancer.

WHATEVER HAPPENED TO . . .

B.F. GOODRICH

— Founded 1870 —

They don't make tires anymore, just chemicals like polyvinyl chloride (PVC), a plastic used in many products. But Goodrich tires are still made—by France's Michelin.

5 U.S. Stocks You Should Have Bought in 1990

Dell (DELL), based in Round Rock, Texas, is the number one maker of computers.

$1,000 invested in Dell shares on the first trading day of 1990 would have escalated to $670,604 by March 31, 2005.

EMC (EMC), based in Hopkinton, Massachusetts, makes information storage and management systems where companies can park their data.

$1,000 invested in EMC shares on the first trading day of 1990 would have jumped to $185,756 by March 31, 2005.

Best Buy (BBY), based in Richfield, Minnesota, operates the nation's largest chain of electronics stores (more than 700 in the United States and Canada).

$1,000 invested in Best Buy shares at the start of 1990 would have increased in value to $164,464 by March 31, 2005.

UnitedHealth Group (UNH) is a Minnesota-based health care plan provider.

$1,000 invested in shares of UNH on the first trading day of 1990 would have grown to $127,041 by March 31, 2005.

Electronic Arts (ERTS), based in Redwood City, California, is one of the world's top video game producers (*The Sims*, *Madden NFL*, *Need for Speed*).

$1,000 invested in Electronic Arts shares at the beginning of 1990 would have been worth $90,792 by March 31, 2005.

5 U.S. Stocks You Should Have Avoided in 1990

Ebix (EBIX), based in Schaumburg, Illinois, is a provider of software and online services for the insurance industry.

$1,000 invested in Ebix shares on the first trading day of 1990 would have plunged to $37.52 by March 31, 2005.

Interland (INLD), based in Atlanta, Georgia, provides Internet hosting services for small and midsized companies.

$1,000 invested in Interland shares at the beginning of 1990 would have dropped to $53.50 by March 31, 2005.

Galaxy Nutritional Foods (GXY), based in Orlando, Florida, supplies grocers with soy-based alternatives to dairy products (milk, cheese, butter).

$1,000 invested in Galaxy shares on the first trading day of 1990 descended to $65.71 by March 31, 2005.

Canyon Resources (CAU), based in Golden, Colorado, operates gold and silver mines.

$1,000 invested in Canyon shares on the first trading day of 1990 was worth $67.75 by March 31, 2005.

NeoRx (NERX), based in Seattle, Washington, is a biotech company trying to develop cancer-fighting drugs.

$1,000 invested in NeoRx shares at the start of 1990 declined to $70.71 by March 31, 2005.

Note: Final return assumes that all dividends and distributions were reinvested in stock.

IN THE IMMORTAL WORDS OF . . .

"What do you do when your competitor is drowning? Find a live hose and stick it in his mouth."

—M. DOUGLAS IVESTER,
CEO OF COCA-COLA, 1997–2000

The Incestuous Automobile Industry

Ford owns Jaguar, Volvo cars, Aston Martin, and Land Rover, and holds a 33 percent stake in Mazda. General Motors owns Saab and Opel, 12 percent of Isuzu, 20 percent of Suzuki, and has a joint venture with Toyota in a California plant that produces Corollas and Pontiac Vibes. Suzuki controls Indian carmaker Maruti Udyog and has a joint venture with Hungarian carmaker Autokonszern. Fiat controls Alfa Romeo, Ferrari, Maserati, and Lancia. Nissan owns 15 percent of Renault, and Renault owns 44 percent of Nissan and 99.3 percent of Romanian car producer Dacia. DaimlerChrysler controls Detroit Diesel. Toyota owns 5 percent of Yamaha and 50.1 percent of truck maker Hino. Citroën, now part of Peugeot, has a joint venture with Toyota to produce cars in the Czech Republic. Volkswagen owns Audi, Skoda, Bugatti, Lamborghini, SEAT, and Bentley. BMW owns Rolls-Royce and MINI.

Match the Company with Nationality of the Owner

1. Nestlé
2. H&M
3. Westinghouse
4. Four Seasons
5. Jaguar
6. Nokia
7. Zara
8. 7-Eleven
9. Ben & Jerry's
10. LensCrafters
11. Maybelline
12. Beringer

a. **Germany**
b. **Italy**
c. **France**
d. **Switzerland**
e. **Sweden**
f. **Australia**
g. **Japan**
h. **United States**
i. **Finland**
j. **United Kingdom**
k. **Spain**
l. **Canada**

ANSWERS: 1d; 2e; 3a; 4l; 5h; 6i; 7k; 8g; 9j; 10b; 11c; 12f

WHATEVER HAPPENED TO . . .

AMERICAN CAN

— FOUNDED 1901 —

This pillar of the old industrial order went downhill in the 1980s and morphed into financial services as Primerica, which was Sandy Weill's platform for the eventual takeover of Citigroup. Its original can-making business ended up in the hands of French metals giant Pechiney.

World's 50 Largest Companies*

Company	Country	Sales
1. Wal-Mart	U.S.	$285.2 billion
2. BP	UK	$285.0 billion
3. Royal Dutch/Shell	Netherlands/UK	$265.1 billion
4. ExxonMobil	U.S.	$263.9 billion
5. General Motors	U.S.	$193.4 billion
6. DaimlerChrysler	Germany	$192.7 billion
7. Ford Motor	U.S.	$170.8 billion
8. Toyota	Japan	$165.6 billion
9. General Electric	U.S.	$152.3 billion
10. Chevron	U.S.	$142.9 billion
11. Total	France	$131.6 billion
12. Volkswagen	Germany	$120.7 billion
13. ConocoPhillips	U.S.	$118.7 billion
14. Allianz	Germany	$112.3 billion
15. Citigroup	U.S.	$108.2 billion
16. Nippon Telegraph & Telephone	Japan	$106.3 billion
17. AXA	France	$97.9 billion
18. IBM	U.S.	$96.3 billion
19. AIG	U.S.	$95.0 billion
20. Siemens	Germany	$93.4 billion
21. ING	Netherlands	$92.0 billion
22. Carrefour	France	$88.6 billion
23. Hitachi	Japan	$82.7 billion

Company	Country	Sales
24. Hewlett-Packard	U.S.	$81.8 billion
25. ENI	Italy	$79.3 billion
26. Honda	Japan	$78.2 billion
27. McKesson	U.S.	$77.8 billion
28. Peugeot	France	$77.0 billion
29. Berkshire Hathaway	U.S.	$74.2 billion
30. Generali	Italy	$73.2 billion
31. Home Depot	U.S.	$73.0 billion
32. Sony	Japan	$71.8 billion
33. Matsushita	Japan	$71.6 billion
34. Verizon	U.S.	$71.2 billion
35. Nissan	Japan	$71.1 billion
36. Nestlé	Switzerland	$70.9 billion
37. Ahold	Netherlands	$70.5 billion
38. Deutsche Telekom	Germany	$70.2 billion
39. Cardinal Health	U.S.	$69.6 billion
40. Metro AG	Germany	$67.4 billion
41. IFIL	Italy	$65.9 billion
42. Bank of America	U.S.	$65.4 billion
43. Aviva	UK	$64.6 billion
44. France Telecom	France	$63.9 billion
45. Altria	U.S.	$63.9 billion
46. Crédit Agricole	France	$63.3 billion
47. HSBC	UK	$62.9 billion
48. Fortis	Netherlands/Belgium	$62.2 billion
49. UBS	Switzerland	$62.2 billion
50. Vodafone	UK	$61.9 billion

**Ranked by 2004 sales*

(Continued on page 60)

(Continued from page 59)

TOP 50 BREAKDOWN

By Nationality	By Industry
American: 18	Automotive: 8
Japanese: 7	Oil and gas: 7
French: 6	Insurance: 6
German: 6	Retail: 5
British: 4	Telecom: 5
Italian: 3	Banking: 4
Dutch: 2	High-tech/electronics: 4
Swiss: 2	Conglomerates: 4
Belgian-Dutch: 1	Diversified financial services: 3
Anglo-Dutch: 1	Wholesalers/healthcare: 2
	Food and beverage: 1
	Tobacco: 1

Top-Selling Liquor Brands in the United States

	Annual Case Sales
1. Bacardi rum	8.5 million
2. Smirnoff vodka	7.3 million
3. Captain Morgan rum	4.8 million
4. Absolut vodka	4.6 million
5. Jack Daniel's bourbon	4.2 million
6. Crown Royal whiskey	3.5 million
7. Jose Cuervo tequila	3.4 million
8. Jim Beam bourbon	3.2 million
9. De Kuyper liqueur	2.8 million
10. Seagram gin	2.7 million

Sony Founder Explains Why Pearl Harbor Was Attacked

TO THE WORLD AT LARGE, Akio Morita, cofounder of Sony Corporation, was undoubtedly the most well-known Japanese business executive of the post–World War II era. He was the face of Sony for many years. He went to New York in 1953 to pay Western Electric $25,000 for rights to the transistor technology, and in 1960 he took up residence in an apartment at the ritzy address of 1010 Fifth Avenue. A year later he arranged for Sony stock to be traded on the U.S. over-the-counter market, the first Japanese company with such a listing. And in 1970 Sony became the first Japanese company to be listed on the New York Stock Exchange.

Akio Morita

Morita held strong opinions and was not bashful about expressing them. For example, in his 1986 autobiography, *Made in Japan*, he speculated that Americans have a soft spot in their hearts for the underdog. One result, he added, was this:

> American sympathy for China's Chiang Kai-Shek as the underdog in the war with Japan (dramatized by his charming American-educated, English-speaking wife) turned into a national consensus that eventually helped to drive the United States and Japan toward war.

Akio Morita died in 1999 at age 78.

Top 5 U.S. Newspapers

	SUNDAY/WEEKEND CIRCULATION*
USA Today	2,612,946
Wall Street Journal	2,070,498
New York Times	1,680,582
Los Angeles Times	1,253,849
Washington Post	1,000,565

**Average Sunday circulation in six months, ending March 2005; figures for* USA Today *and* Wall Street Journal *are for Friday editions*

The *New York Times* was the only one of the five national newspapers to show a recognizable increase for the period from September 2004 to March 2005, a puny gain of two-tenths of 1 percent.

ABOUT 314 ACRES OF TREES ARE USED TO MAKE THE NEWSPRINT FOR THE AVERAGE SUNDAY EDITION OF THE *NEW YORK TIMES*.

The New York Times Company does more than publish the *New York Times*. It publishes 18 other newspapers, including the *Boston Globe*, *Sarasota Herald-Tribune*, and *Press-Democrat* in Santa Rosa, California; owns eight TV stations, including KFOR in Oklahoma City and WHO in Des Moines; and owns two New York City radio stations. It also holds a 17 percent stake in New England Sports Ventures, owner of the Boston Red Sox and the legendary Fenway Park.

GENERAL ELECTRIC BUYS LIABILITY INSURANCE FOR ITS OFFICERS AND MEMBERS OF ITS BOARD OF DIRECTORS. ANNUAL PREMIUMS FOR THIS COVERAGE: $22.4 MILLION.

General Electric, Relentless Shopper

ACQUISITIONS, DECEMBER 2003–NOVEMBER 2004	**PURCHASE PRICE**
IKON (office equipment leasing)	$1.9 billion
AstroPower (solar panels)	$18.5 million
InVision (security scanners)	$900 million
Boeing Capital (commercial finance)	$1.7 billion
Mervyn's (credit cards)	$475 million
Hyundai Capital Services (commercial finance)	$375 million
Dillard National (credit cards)	$1.25 billion
BHA (air pollution controls)	$260 million
Australian Financial (mortgages)	$400 million
Deltabank (Russian credit cards)	$120 million
Edwards Systems Technology (fire detection)	$1.4 billion
CrossCountry Energy (gas pipelines)	$1.2 billion
CitiCapital (truck leasing)	$4.4 billion
Ionics (water treatment)	$1.3 billion
Others (including ChevronTexaco clean coal technology, SD Myers, WMC, RD Lizinga)	$800 million

TOTAL: $16.5 billion

15 Largest U.S. Employers in 2004

	EMPLOYEES*
1. Wal-Mart	1.7 million
2. McDonald's	438,000
3. United Parcel Service	384,000
4. Sears Holdings	380,000
5. IBM	369,000
6. Home Depot	325,000
7. Ford	324,850
8. General Motors	324,000
9. General Electric	307,000
10. Citigroup	294,000
11. Target	292,000
12. Kroger	289,000
13. Albertson's	241,000
14. Verizon	210,000
15. United Technologies	209,700

**Worldwide totals*

Supersize Me

The world's largest McDonald's is located in Beijing, China. This two-story, 28,000-square-foot (0.3-hectare) facility seats 700 and employs 1,000.

The world's largest hotelkeeper is Marriott, which was started in 1927 as an A&W Root Beer stand in Washington, D.C. The company has more than 2,600 properties in the United States and 65 other countries. Every day it has 374,000 rooms to rent in the United States. It owns the Ritz-Carlton and Renaissance chains in addition to the Marriott hotels. Courtyard and Fairfield Inn are also Marriott hotel brands.

TOP 10

Places to Work in the United States

	2004	2005	2006
1.	J.M. Smucker	Wegmans	Genentech
2.	Alston & Bird	W.L. Gore	Wegmans
3.	Container Store	Republic Bancorp	Valero Energy
4.	Edward Jones	Genentech	Griffin Hospital
5.	Republic Bancorp	Xilinx	W.L. Gore
6.	Adobe Systems	J.M. Smucker	Container Store
7.	TDIndustries	SC Johnson	Vision Service Plan
8.	SAS Institute	Griffin Hospital	J.M. Smucker
9.	Wegmans	Alston & Bird	REI
10.	Xilinx	Vision Service Plan	S.C. Johnson

The Saga of American Department Stores

1830 Shillito's founded in Cincinnati by John Shillito.

1841 Eben Jordan and Benjamin L. Marsh open Jordan Marsh in Boston.

1851 F&R Lazarus founded in Columbus, Ohio, by Simon Lazarus.

1858 Rowland H. Macy opens R. H. Macy as a dry goods store in New York City. First day sales: $11.06.

1865 Wechsler & Abraham (later Abraham & Straus) founded in Brooklyn, New York, by Joseph Wechsler and Abraham Abraham.

1867 Rich's founded in Atlanta by Morris Rich.

1867 Stern Brothers (later Stern's) founded in Manhattan.

1870 Goldsmith's founded in Memphis.

1872 Bloomingdale Brothers founded in New York City by Lyman and Joseph Bloomingdale. First day sales: $3.68.

1888 Straus family forms a partnership with Macy's.

1890 Bon Marche founded in Seattle.

1893 Straus family buys out Joseph Wechsler's interest in Wechsler & Abraham, changing store's name to Abraham & Straus.

1898 Burdine's founded in Miami.

1902 Macy's moves to Herald Square in New York City.

1907 Bullock's founded by John Bullock and P. G. Winnett in Los Angeles.

1924 Expanding to 7th Avenue, Macy's Herald Square location becomes largest store in the world. A crowd of 10,000 watch Macy's first Thanksgiving Day Parade.

1925 Macy's acquires Davison-Paxon-Stokes of Atlanta.

1929 Family-owned department stores—Abraham & Straus, Lazarus, Filene's in Boston—organize Federated Department Stores as a holding company, with headquarters in Columbus, Ohio.

1930 Bloomingdale's joins Federated. First-year sales for Federated: $112 million.

1935 Another holding company, Allied Stores, founded in New York. Members included Jordan Marsh and Hahn department stores.

1935 Fred Lazarus Jr. persuades President Franklin D. Roosevelt to change the Thanksgiving Day holiday from the last Thursday of November to the fourth Thursday, thereby extending the Christmas shopping season. A 1941 Act of Congress perpetuated this arrangement.

(Continued on page 68)

(Continued from page 67)

1939 Federated and Allied stores begin offering credit terms to customers.

1945 Federated moves its offices to Cincinnati. Macy's acquires O'Connor Moffat of San Francisco.

1946 Shillito's becomes the first American department store to reach out to the African-American community, offering credit to blacks and employing them as salespeople and executives. The store's restaurant is the first in downtown Cincinnati to serve African-American customers.

1947 O'Connor Moffat in San Francisco renamed Macy's California.

1951 Allied Stores acquires New Jersey's Stern Brothers.

1956 Miami-based Burdine's becomes a division of Federated.

1957 Seventeen-year-old Ralph Lauren (born in the Bronx in 1939 as Ralph Lifshitz) begins to sell sweaters at Bloomingdale's over Christmas week.

1958 Ralph Lauren joins Allied Stores as assistant menswear buyer.

1959 Federated acquires Rike's, based in Dayton, Ohio, and Memphis-based Goldsmith's.

1962 Allied Stores acquires Wiliam H. Block of Indianapolis.

1964 Federated, crossing the $1 billion sales mark for the first time, acquires two California department store chains—Bullock's and I. Magnin.

1967 Allied Stores passes the $1 billion sales mark.

1968 Abraham & Straus executives play lead role in formation of the Black Retail Action Group (BRAG) to give technical assistance to minority-owned businesses and to offer scholarships to minority retailing students.

1976 Federated acquires Atlanta-based Rich's.

1980 Federated sets up $15 million foundation.

1982 Rike's of Dayton merges with Cincinnati's Shillito's.

1985 Davison's of Atlanta changes name to Macy's.

1986 Shillito's-Rikes merges with Lazarus; the surviving entity carries the Lazarus name.

1986 Canadian real estate developer Robert Campeau, borrowing from Canadian banks and investors, buys Allied Stores, then the fifth largest U.S. department store group, operating stores under 16 different names.

1987 Federated buys Indianapolis-based Block's from Allied Stores, folding it into the Lazarus chain.

1988 Campeau acquires Federated Department Stores, then the largest U.S. department store group, operating stores under 17 different names. Several Federated entities, including Foley's and Filene's, are sold off. Macy's buys Bullock's and I. Magnin from Campeau. Allied Stores closes its New York headquarters, merging into Federated's base in Cincinnati.

(Continued on page 70)

(Continued from page 69)

1990 Struggling under a debt burden of $8 billion, the Campeau adventure unravels. Both Federated and Allied Stores file for bankruptcy protection. The *New York Times* comments: "Any corporate executive can figure out how to file for bankruptcy when the bottom drops out of the business. It took the special genius of Robert Campeau to figure out how to bankrupt more than 250 profitable department stores. The dramatic jolt to Bloomingdale's, Abraham & Straus, Jordan Marsh, and the other proud stores reflects his overreaching grasp and oversized ego."

1991 Still operating under bankruptcy, Federated consolidates all its Jordan Marsh and Maas Brothers stores in Florida under the Burdine's name.

1992 Federated Department Stores emerges from bankruptcy as a new public company operating 220 department stores in 26 states, with total sales of $7 billion. The old Allied Stores group is merged into Federated.

1992 Macy's, saddled with a huge debt as a result of top executives buying the company and taking it private, files for bankruptcy protection.

1994 Federated acquires Macy's and Joseph Horne of Pittsburgh and discontinues the I. Magnin chain.

1995 Rich's/Goldsmith's and Lazarus are consolidated into one division. Federated acquires Los Angeles–based Broadway Stores, which operated 82 stores under the Broadway, Emporium, and Weinstock's names. Fifty-six of the stores are immediately converted to the Macy's nameplate, five become Bloomingdale's; the others are shuttered. In the East, Abraham & Straus stores become Macy's stores.

1996 Jordan Marsh stores in the Northeast are converted to the Macy's nameplate. Bullock's stores in Southern California become Macy's stores. Bloomingdale's opens its first California stores—three in the Los Angeles area, one in Palo Alto.

1999 Federated acquires Fingerhut, a Minnesota catalog seller.

2001 Federated closes Stern's, converting most stores to the Bloomingdale's or Macy's nameplates.

2002 Federated disposes of Fingerhut.

2003 Federated integrates the Macy's name with its regional stores, creating Bon-Macy's, Burdines-Macy's, Goldsmith's-Macy's, Lazarus-Macy's and Rich's-Macy's. Bloomingdale's enters the Atlanta market with two stores.

2005 Federated begins operating nationwide under two national brands: Macy's and Bloomingdale's. All the other local names are scuttled. Federated acquires May Department stores, operator of 950 stores in 64 major metropolitan centers. Names scheduled to join the Federated roster: Famous-Barr, Filene's, Foley's, Hecht's, Kaufmann's, Lord & Taylor, L.S. Ayers, Marshall Field's, Meier & Frank, Robinsons-May, Strawbridge's, the Jones Stores. At the time of publication, all former May stores, with the exception of Lord & Taylor, are scheduled to convert to the Macy's nameplate.

* * *

How Companies Divided Their Political Contributions in the 2004 U.S. Election

	REPUBLICANS	DEMOCRATS
Wal-Mart	78%	22%
Starbucks	—	100%
Anheuser-Busch	56%	44%
Hallmark Cards	81%	19%
Clear Channel	67%	33%
Bed Bath & Beyond	3%	97%
Procter & Gamble	79%	21%
Progressive Insurance	9%	91%
JC Penney	88%	12%
Apple Computer	19%	81%
Dunkin' Donuts	88%	12%
Costco	1%	99%
Geico	95%	5%
Dell Computer	77%	22%
Tommy Hilfiger	9%	91%
Calvin Klein	—	100%
Estée Lauder	5%	95%
Levi Strauss	3%	97%
Circuit City	95%	5%
Gallo Winery	5%	95%

	REPUBLICANS	DEMOCRATS
Coors	92%	8%
K-mart	70%	30%
Kohler	100%	—
Target	70%	30%
3M	70%	30%
Home Depot	89%	11%
Amway	100%	—
McDonald's	86%	14%
Marriott	81%	19%
Hyatt	20%	80%
Outback Steakhouse	95%	5%

WHATEVER HAPPENED TO . . .

International Harvester

— Founded 1902 —

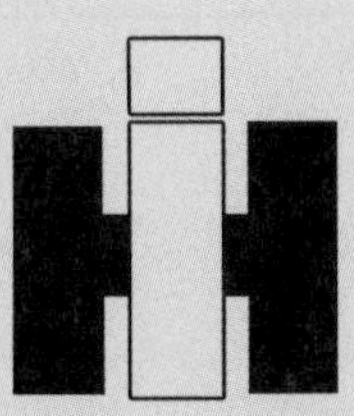

This pioneer in agricultural equipment—and stalwart of the Chicago business establishment—bit the dust in the 1980s, the victim of a bloated bureaucracy and a 172-day strike by the UAW. Competitors scooped up the farming products, and the truck division survived under a new name, Navistar. Memorabilia totaling 12 million manuscript pages, 250,000 photographs, 300 films, and thousands of other items (books, newspapers, machines, toys, clothing) were donated to the State Historical Society of Wisconsin in Madison.

5 European Stocks You Should Have Bought in 1990

Sage Group (SGE), headquartered in Newcastle Upon Tyne, England, develops software for business customers.

€1,000 invested in Sage shares at the end of 1989 would have appreciated to €77,688 by March 31, 2005.

London-based **CAPITA GROUP** (CPI) provides professional services for companies outsourcing departments such as human resources and back office processes.

€1,000 invested in Capita Group at the start of 1990 would have escalated to €75,087 by March 31, 2005.

Metka (METKK), part of the Greek conglomerate Mytilineos Group, based in Athens, is a metal construction company.

€1,000 invested in Metka shares at the start of 1990 would have increased to €42,776 by March 31, 2005.

Kingspan Group (KGP), based in County Cavan in Ireland, makes a wide range of products—insulated panels, flooring, roofs—used in the construction industry.

€1,000 invested in Kingspan shares at the start of 1990 would have increased in value to €39,734 by March 31, 2005.

Zeltia (ZEL), based in Madrid, makes chemical and pharmaceutical products.

€1,000 invested in Zeltia at the end of 1989 would have grown to €29,730 by March 31, 2005.

5 European Stocks You Should Have Avoided in 1990

Smart Approach (LWE), based in the Lincolnshire town of Grimsby, designs training software used in the aviation and other security markets.

€1,000 invested in Smart Approach at the end of 1989 would have eroded to €8.24 by March 31, 2005.

BioPorto (THOR-B), based in Gentofte, Denmark, invests in biotechnology startups.

€1,000 invested in BioPorto shares at the start of 1990 would have eroded to €8.32 by March 31, 2005.

Baumwollspinnerei Gronau (BSO), headquartered in Gronau, Germany, spins yarns and threads used to make worsted carpets.

€1,000 invested in BSO shares at the end of 1989 would have declined to €8.96 by March 31, 2005.

London-based **Maisha** (MSA) sells Royal Jelly products.

€1,000 invested in Maisha at the end of 1989 would have plunged to €9.35 on March 31, 2005.

London-based **Parallel Media Group** (OFU) lines up corporate sponsors for sports teams.

€1,000 invested in Parallel Media shares at the start of 1990 would have ended up worth €12.13 by March 31, 2005.

Note: Final return assumes that all dividends and distributions were reinvested in stock.

*Top 25 Soccer Teams by Market Value**

TEAM & COUNTRY	VALUE 2005	REVENUES (2003–04 SEASON)
1. **Manchester United** England	$1.2 billion	$315 million
2. **Real Madrid** Spain	$920 million	$287 million
3. **AC Milan** Italy	$893 million	$270 million
4. **Juventus** Italy	$837 million	$262 million
5. **Bayern Munich** Germany	$627 million	$202 million
6. **Arsenal** England	$613 million	$211 million
7. **Internzionale Milan** Italy	$608 million	$203 million
8. **Chelsea** England	$449 million	$264 million
9. **Liverpool** England	$441 million	$170 million
10. **Newcastle United** England	$391 million	$166 million
11. **Barcelona** Spain	$389 million	$206 million

TEAM & COUNTRY	VALUE 2005	REVENUES (2003–04 SEASON)
12. Olympique Marseille France	$305 million	$107 million
13. Tottenham Hotspur England	$298 million	$122 million
14. Schalke 04 Germany	$295 million	$111 million
15. Celtic Scotland	$273 million	$127 million
16. Manchester City England	$262 million	$114 million
17. AS Roma Italy	$252 million	$132 million
18. Aston Villa England	$236 million	$103 million
19. Glasgow Rangers Scotland	$225 million	$105 million
20. SS Lazio Italy	$224 million	$121 million
21. Olympique Lyonnais France	$209 million	$139 million
22. Borussia Dortmund Germany	$197 million	$119 million
23. FC Porto Portugal	$182 million	$140 million
24. Leeds United England	$135 million	$85 million
25. Ajax Amsterdam Holland	$126 million	$78 million

**Value of team is based on 2005 stadium deal*

Sins of the Father . . .

JPMORGAN CHASE, the third largest bank in the United States, has a lot of ancestors—and now it's making amends for two of them.

Between 1831 and 1865, two predecessor banks, Citizens Bank and Canal Bank, both operating in Louisiana, apparently made loans with some 13,000 slaves as collateral. When plantation owners defaulted on the loans, the banks took possession of 1,250 slaves. When this history came to light, JPMorgan Chase apologized on its Web site and established a $5 million scholarship fund for African-American college students.

The information originally surfaced as a result of a regulation established in 2002 by the Chicago City Council requiring companies doing business with the city to disclose whether they profited from slavery. After looking at records stored at Tulane University, 12 historians spent more than 3,500 hours researching property and bank records in 39 Louisiana parishes, where the incriminating evidence was discovered.

GENERAL ELECTRIC—ticker symbol GE—is the most widely held stock in the world. The company has some 5 million shareholders, 42 percent of them individuals. GE has about 10.6 billion shares outstanding.

$1,000 invested in GE stock in 1993 would have multiplied to $5,250 by the end of 2004 (assuming reinvestment of all dividends). If you bought one share of stock before 1926, you would have had 4,608 shares in 2005, after all the stock splits.

Club Med, founded as a nonprofit communal summer camp in Majorca, was transformed into a worldwide, profitable chain of resorts by Gilbert Trigano, the son of Algerian Jews. Trigano fought in the Communist resistance during World War II and then wrote for the Communist daily, *L'Humanité*, before taking over Club Med, changing the tents to Polynesian-style huts, and introducing a culture where people were free to take off their clothes (and inhibitions) and have a good time.

Gilbert Trigano

TOP 10 Richest Americans*

1.	**Bill Gates**, cofounder of Microsoft	$51.0 billion
2.	**Warren Buffett**, CEO, Berkshire Hathaway	$41.0 billion
3.	**Paul Allen**, cofounder of Microsoft	$22.5 billion
4.	**Michael Dell**, founder of Dell Computer	$18.0 billion
5.	**Lawrence Ellison**, founder of Oracle	$17.0 billion
6.	**Jim C. Walton**, son of Sam Walton	$15.7 billion
7.	**Christy Walton**, daughter-in-law of Sam Walton	$15.7 billion
8.	**S. Robson Walton**, son of Sam Walton	$15.6 billion
9.	**Alice C. Walton**, daughter of Sam Walton	$15.5 billion
10.	**Helen R. Walton**, widow of Sam Walton	$15.4 billion

**2005 ranking by* Forbes *magazine*

WOMEN NOW ACCOUNT FOR 17 PERCENT OF PARTNERS AT U.S. LAW FIRMS—UP FIVE PERCENTAGE POINTS FROM 10 YEARS AGO.

World's 15 Largest Employers, Determined by Number of Employees

COMPANY	EMPLOYEES
1. Wal-Mart	1.7 million
2. China National Petroleum	1.1 million
3. U.S. Postal Service	807,000
4. Sinopec (China Petroleum & Chemical Corp.)	774,000
5. State Grid (Chinese power utility)	729,327
6. UES (Russian power utility)	496,300
7. Agricultural Bank of China	489,425
8. McDonald's	438,000
9. Carrefour (French retailer)	436,000
10. Siemens (German electrical engineering and electronics)	430,000
11. China Telecommunications	406,000
12. Compass Group (UK foodservice company)	402,375
13. Gazprom (Russian natural gas producer)	388,714
14. DaimlerChrysler	384,723
15. United Parcel Service	384,000

Taking Care of the People at the Top

When Procter & Gamble of Cincinnati acquired Gillette of Boston in 2005, the top executives of Gillette became eligible for severance payments and other benefits to compensate them for the disruption of their careers.

The top five Gillette executives were slated for the following payouts:

James M. Kilts, CEO: **$164 million**
Edward F. DeGraan, vice chairman: **$45 million**
Charles W. Cramb, senior vice president: **$26 million**
Peter K. Hoffman, vice president: **$20 million**
Mark M. Leckie, vice president: **$17 million**

Twelve other executive officers became eligible for payouts totaling $175,868,872. "Other key Gillette employees" terminated for good reason within the first two years after the merger would be eligible for severance payments of two times the employee's base salary and bonus.

No word about any provisions for the 28,000 Gillette employees below these management honchos.

Tail Wagging the Dog

2004 U.S. Box Office Movie Revenues	$9.53 billion
2004 U.S. DVD Sales and Rentals	$16 billion
2004 U.S. VHS Sales and Rentals	$10 billion

PROFILE

Cargill

MOST PEOPLE have never heard of Cargill, despite its enormous size (nearly $63 billion in annual revenues), reach (101,000 employees on four continents), and influence (it sets the terms of agricultural transactions). This company you've never heard of is larger than JPMorgan Chase, Kroger, Procter & Gamble, Boeing, and Johnson & Johnson, and twice the size of PepsiCo, DuPont, JC Penney, and Goldman Sachs.

Headquartered in a faux French chateau 25 miles from downtown Minneapolis, Minnesota, Cargill helps farmers grow crops, stores their output in grain elevators, sells it to food producers around the world, and offers a raft of ancillary services and products ranging from steel (it has its own mills) to commodity trading. In recent years it has branched out from its middleman role to become a processor of foods that it markets under its own brand names. Among its brands are Burrus Flour, Diamond Crystal Salt, Nutrena Feeds, Gerkens Cocoa, Honeysuckle White Turkey, and Sterling Silver Fresh Meats.

As a privately owned company, Cargill does not have to disclose information that publicly traded companies are required to detail. However, in 2004 it opened its doors a crack to *Financial Times* writer Caroline Daniel, who presented this assessment of Cargill's power:

- It controls 25 percent of all U.S. grain exports.
- It holds about 22 percent of the U.S. meat market, equivalent to processing 22,500 cattle a day.
- It accounts for 21 percent of U.S. turkey production.
- It controls 9 percent of the U.S. pork market.
- It's the largest exporter from Argentina.
- It's the biggest poultry processor in Thailand.

- It supplies all the eggs used in McDonald's stores in the United States.
- It supplies much of the sugar used by Coca-Cola.

Cargill is one of the oldest companies in America. It was founded in 1865 in Conover, Iowa, by two brothers, William and Samuel Cargill, sons of a Scottish sea captain. Their original business was a grain warehouse. The family has two branches, the Cargills and the MacMillans, and together they still control about 85 percent of the stock of this enormous company.

Drugs Around the World

Worldwide sales of pharmaceuticals passed the $500 billion mark in 2004. These sales were divided geographically as follows:

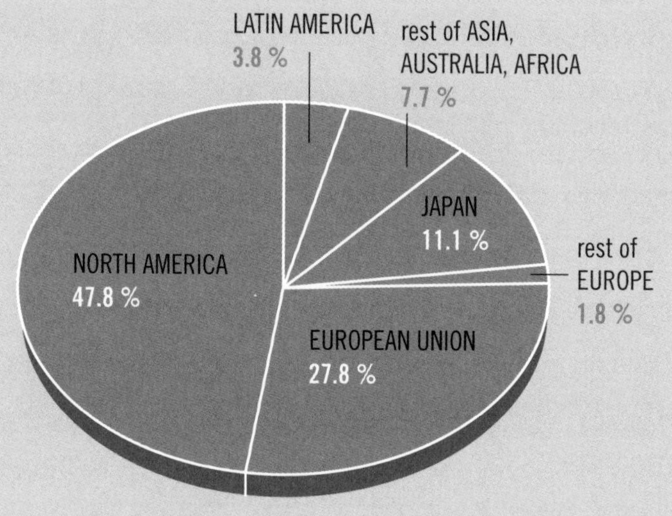

5 U.S. Stocks You Should Have Bought in 1995

NVR (NVR), based in Reston, Virginia, builds homes under the Ryan, Fox Ridge, and NV names.

$1,000 invested in NVR shares on the first day of trading in 1995 would have escalated to $142,727 by March 31, 2005.

Chico's FAS (CHS), based in Fort Myers, Florida, operates 670 apparel and accessories stores in 47 states under the names Chico's, White House, Black Market, Soma, and Chico's Outlet.

$1,000 invested in Chico's stock in the beginning of 1995 would have been worth $101,735 by March 31, 2005.

Biogen Idec (BIIB), based in Cambridge, Massachusetts, is a biotech drug company whose lineup includes Rituxan, used to treat lymphomas, and Avonex, used to treat multiple sclerosis.

$1,000 invested in Biogen shares on the first trading day of 1995 would have grown to $97,440 by March 31, 2005.

Apollo Group (APOL), based in Phoenix, Arizona, operates the University of Phoenix, the nation's largest private university, offering courses online and at 100 learning centers and 50 campuses.

$1,000 invested in Apollo shares on the first trading day of 1995 would have jumped to $94,719 by March 31, 2005.

QLogic (QLGC), based in Aliso Viejo, California, designs network storage equipment such as switches and controllers.

$1,000 invested in QLogic shares on the first trading day of 1995 would have grown to $48,000 by March 31, 2005.

5 U.S. Stocks You Should Have Avoided in 1995

Irvine Sensors (IRSN), based in Costa Mesa, California, supplies lightweight, solid-state microcircuits primarily to the United States and its military contractors.

$1,000 invested in Irvine Sensors shares on the first trading day of 1995 would have declined to $17.83 by March 31, 2005.

Universal Automotive Industries (UVSL), based in Alsip, Illinois, makes auto parts such as brake drums, shoes, and disc pads.

$1,000 invested in Universal Automotive shares at the start of 1995 would have been worth $18 on March 31, 2005.

Genta (GNTA), based in Berkeley Heights, New Jersey, is a biotech company trying to develop anti-cancer drugs.

$1,000 invested in Genta shares on the first trading day of 1995 would have declined to $22.05 by March 31, 2005.

North American Technologies (NATK), based in Houston, Texas, makes composite railroad ties made of recycled plastic and rubber (TieTek).

$1,000 invested in North American Technologies shares on the first trading day of 1995 descended to $29.04 by March 31, 2005.

Suntron (SUNN), based in Phoenix, Arizona, is a contract manufacturer of electronic components such as printed circuit boards, cables, and harnesses.

$1,000 invested in Suntron shares at the start of 1995 would have eroded to $70.49 by March 31, 2005.

Note: Final return assumes that all dividends and distributions were reinvested in stock.

World's Top 50 Restaurants*

1. The Fat Duck	Bray, England
2. El Bulli	Montjoi Girona, Spain
3. The French Laundry	Yountville, California
4. Tetsuya's	Sydney, Australia
5. Gordon Ramsay	London
6. Pierre Gagnaire	Paris
7. Per Se	New York
8. Tom Aikens	London
9. Jean Georges	New York
10. St. John	London
11. Michel Bras	Laguiole, France
12. Le Louis XV	Monte Carlo, Monaco
13. Chez Panisse	Berkeley, California
14. Charlie Trotter's	Chicago
15. Gramercy Tavern	New York
16. Guy Savoy	Paris
17. Alain Ducasse (Plaza Athénée)	Paris
18. The Gallery at Sketch	London
19. The Waterside Inn	Bray, England
20. Nobu	London
21. Arzak	San Sebastian, Spain
22. Can Fabes	San Celoni, Spain
23. Checchino dal 1887	Rome

24. Le Meurice	Paris
25. L'Hôtel de Ville	Crissier, Switzerland
26. L'Arpège	Paris
27. Angela Hartnett (The Connaught)	London
28. Le Manoir aux Quat' Saisons	Oxford, England
29. Le Cinq	Paris
30. Hakkasan	London
31. Cal Pep	Barcelona
32. Masa	New York
33. Flower Drum	Melbourne, Australia
34. wd-50	New York
35. Le Quartier Français	Franschhoek, South Africa
36. Spice Market	New York
37. Auberge de l'Ill	Illhaeusern, France
38. Manresa	Los Gatos, California
39. Dieter Muller	Bergisch Gladbach, Germany
40. La Maison Troisgros	Roanne, France
41. The Wolseley	London
42. Rockpool	Sydney, Australia
43. Yauatcha	London
44. The Ivy	London
45. Gambero Rosso	San Vincenzo, Italy
46. The Cliff	St. James, Barbados
47. La Gavroche	London
48. Enoteca Pinchiorri	Florence, Italy
49. Felix	Hong Kong
50. La Tupina	Bordeaux, France

**Chosen in a 2005 survey of chefs, restaurateurs, and food journalists conducted by* Restaurant *magazine*

SINCE THE 1980S, 40 TO 50 PERCENT OF LAW SCHOOL GRADUATES HAVE BEEN WOMEN.

How China's TCL Company Became the World's Largest TV Manufacturer

In 1986, when General Electric bought RCA, the last thing it wanted to do was to make televisions and radios. So it traded this business to the big French electronics company, Thomson, in exchange for Thomson's medical diagnostic business. Thomson struggled to make a go of it in television set manufacturing and virtually threw in the towel in 2003 when it ceded control of its television manufacturing business to a Chinese company, TCL.

Located in the southern China city of Hiuzhou, TCL didn't start to make televisions until 1992. But it ramped up production quickly, shipping more than 11 million sets in 2003, including some 4 million sold overseas under name brands such as Panasonic and Philips. In 2002, it gained its first overseas manufacturing unit by buying the bankrupt German company Schneider Technologies. The 2003 deal with Thomson gave TCL television plants in France, Poland, and Thailand. And it brought into its domain the venerable American brand name RCA, whose sets had been made in Bloomington, Indiana.

Result: TCL is now the number one purveyor of television sets, selling 18 million a year, ahead of Sony, Matsushita (Panasonic), and Samsung.

Where the Oil Is and Who Uses Most of It

Top 11 Countries with Oil Reserves

	Reserves in Billions of Barrels	Percent of World Reserves
Saudi Arabia	262	21.6
Canada	180	14.0
Iraq	113	9.0
United Arab Emirates	98	8.1
Kuwait	97	8.0
Iran	90	7.4
Venezuela	78	6.4
Russia	60	4.9
Libya	30	2.4
Nigeria	24	2.0
United States	23	1.9

Top 11 Consumers of Oil (in millions of barrels per day)

United States	20.1
China	5.6
Japan	5.4
Russia	2.8
Germany	2.6
India	2.2
South Korea	2.2
France	2.1
Canada	2.1
Brazil	2.1
Mexico	2.0

The Mall of America in Bloomington, Minnesota, just outside of Minneapolis, is the size of 78 football fields, or 9.5 million square feet (883,000 sq m).

5 European Stocks You Should Have Bought in 1995

Tandberg (TAA), based in Lysaker, Norway, develops video-conferencing systems and management software.

€1,000 invested in Tandberg shares at the end of 1994 would have leaped to €233,009 by March 31, 2005.

Wembley (WMBYY), a British gaming company based in Wembley, Middlesex, operates greyhound racing tracks in England and the United States.

€1,000 invested in Wembley at the start of 1995 would have grown to €186,774 by March 31, 2005.

Acanthe Developpement (6460) is a French real estate company based in Paris.

€1,000 invested in Acanthe shares at the end of 1994 would have increased to €59,742 by March 31, 2005.

Madrid-based **Testa Inmuebles en Renta** (TST) is a major Spanish real estate developer.

€1,000 invested in Testa shares at the start of 1995 would have appreciated to €55,382 by March 31, 2005.

Altin (ALT), based in Baar, Switzerland, is an investment company.

€1,000 invested in Altin shares at the end of 1994 would have grown to €42,377 by March 31, 2005.

5 European Stocks You Should Have Avoided in 1995

Escom (ECM), based in Bochum, Germany, was once Europe's second largest computer retailer.

€1,000 invested in Escom shares at the start of 1995 would have eroded to €5.08 by March 31, 2005.

Schneider Technologies (SRF), based in Tuerkheim, Germany, is an electronics company that makes TV sets, audio systems, digital telephones, and answering machines.

€1,000 invested in Schneider shares at the end of 1994 would have declined to €10.24 by March 31, 2005.

Goodtech (GOD), based in Sandefjord, Norway, operates water treatment plants and makes products to ensure that water is safe.

€1,000 invested in GOD shares at the start of 1995 would have plunged to €10.67 by March 31, 2005.

Munich-based **Valarte Group** (COS) is an investment company whose holdings include furniture wholesalers, construction service providers, machinery manufacturers, and automotive parts suppliers.

€1,000 invested in Valarte at the end of 1994 would have dissipated to €10.77 by March 31, 2005.

Pinguin Haustechnik (TTB), based in Hamburg, Germany, sells bathrooms and water heating systems as well as providing sanitary outfitting of buildings and ships.

€1,000 invested in TTB shares at the end of 1994 would have ratcheted down to €11.48 by March 31, 2005.

Note: Final return assumes that all dividends and distributions were reinvested in stock.

PROFILE

Wrigley Company

William Wrigley Jr.

WHILE THOMAS ADAMS was the first to make a chicle-based gum, the most successful company to emerge from this field was the Wm. Wrigley Jr. Company. William Wrigley Jr. arrived in Chicago in 1891, when he was 29 years old. He first sold soap, giving away baking powder as a premium, and later he switched to selling the baking powder, giving away chewing gum as a freebie. His business continued to develop, and eventually he just sold the gum.

Wrigley was one of the first of the big advertisers. He placed ads in street cars and subways. He put up billboards along railroad tracks. He lit up Times Square with electric signs. And he was a great believer in free samples. He sent out millions of chewing gum sticks to get people to try them. In the early part of the twentieth century, his company reigned as the largest advertiser in the United States.

Chewing gum got a big boost during World War I, when the U.S. Army made it part of the daily ration. Wrigley also went overseas, selling his gum in more than 35 countries. When he died in 1932, he was one of the ten wealthiest men in the United States.

Wrigley shares have been traded on the New York Stock Exchange since 1923, but the company is still controlled by the Wrigley family. The current CEO, William Wrigley Jr. (above), is the great-grandson of the founder.

For more than 100 years the company stuck to one product: gum. Now that's changed—it bought Velamints from a German company, acquired a Spanish confectionery company, and recently picked up Life Savers and Altoids from Altria Group, parent company of Kraft Foods and Phillip Morris.

The Wrigleys did extend their reach into one other area of American pop culture—baseball. Founder William Wrigley Jr. bought the Chicago Cubs in 1916, and the family ran the baseball team with the same single-minded focus that they employed in business until they sold the team to the Tribune Company in 1981.

Changing Advertising Mix

The traditional advertising media—newspapers, magazines, broadcast television, and radio—took big hits in the period from 1999 to 2004. Over those five years advertising in/on:

Newspapers declined by	**18.8%**
Broadcast television declined by	**15.2%**
Magazines declined by	**9.9%**
Radio declined by	**5.6%**

HERE IS HOW THE 2004 ADVERTISING MONEY WAS SPLIT UP:

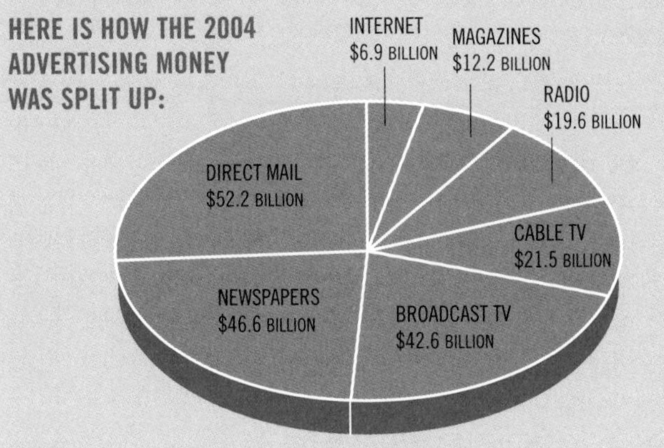

Companies Making Up the Dow Jones Industrial Average

The Original Dow 12 (1897)

American Cotton Oil
American Sugar Refining Company
American Tobacco
Chicago Gas
Distilling & Cattle Feeding Company
General Electric
Laclede Gas Light Company
National Lead
North-American Company
Tennessee Coal, Iron & Railroad Company
U.S. Leather
U.S. Rubber Company

The Dow 20 (1916)

American Beet Sugar
American Can
American Car & Foundry
American Locomotive
American Smelting
American Sugar
American Telephone & Telegraph
Anaconda Copper
Baldwin Locomotive
Central Leather
General Electric
Goodrich
Republic Iron & Steel
Studebaker
Texas Company
U.S. Rubber
U.S. Steel
Utah Copper
Westinghouse
Western Union

The Dow 30 (1928)

Allied Chemical
American Can
American Smelting
American Sugar
American Tobacco
Atlantic Refining
Bethlehem Steel
Chrysler
General Electric
General Motors
General Railway Signal
Goodrich
International Harvester
International Nickel
Mack Truck
Nash Motors
North American
Paramount Publix
Postum Inc.
Radio Corporation of America
Sears, Roebuck
Standard Oil (NJ)
Texas Company
Texas Gulf Sulpher
Union Carbide
U.S. Steel
Victor Talking Machine
Westinghouse Electric
Woolworth
Wright Aeronautical

The Dow 30 (2004)

3M
Alcoa
Altria
American Express
American International Group
Boeing
Caterpillar
Citigroup
Coca-Cola
DuPont
ExxonMobil
General Electric
General Motors
Hewlett-Packard
Home Depot
Honeywell
Intel
International Business Machines
JPMorgan Chase
Johnson & Johnson
McDonald's
Merck
Microsoft
Pfizer
Procter & Gamble
SBC Communications
United Technologies
Verizon
Wal-Mart
Walt Disney

The only company to appear on all lists: General Electric.

Top CEO Golfers*

CEO	HANDICAP	COMPANY
1. Curt Culver	2.4	MGIC (mortgage insurer)
2. Jerry Jurgensen	2.5	Nationwide (insurance)
3. Scott McNealy	2.9	Sun Microsystems (servers)
4. James Blanchard	3.1	Synovus (banking)
5. William Foley	3.8	Fidelity National (insurance)
6. John Lundgren	4.4	Stanley Works (tool maker)
7. Scott Farmer	4.5	Cintas (uniforms)
8. Robert Walter	4.8	Cardinal Health (drug wholesaler)
9. Kenneth Glass	4.9	First Horizon (banking)
10. [Tie]Mayo Shattuck	5.4	Constellation Energy (energy supplier)
David Thomas	5.4	IMS Health (health-care research)

**Based on* Golf Digest's *2004 handicap ranking*

Percentage of shoes sold in the United States that are made in the United States:

1%

Percentage of socks sold in the United States that are made in the United States:

31%

THE WORLD'S LARGEST CONTAINERSHIP OPERATOR IS DENMARK'S MAERSK.

TOP 10

Richest Residents of the UK*

1. **Lakshmi Mittal**, steel magnate	$28.3 [£14.8] BILLION
2. **Roman Abramovich**, Russian business tycoon, owns Chelsea football team	$14.3 [£7.5] BILLION
3. **Duke of Westminster**, owns vast property holdings	$10.7 [£5.6] BILLION
4. **Hans Rausing family**, Swede whose father founded packaging giant Tetra Pak (now Tetra Laval)	$9.4 [£4.95] BILLION
5. **Philip and Christina Green**, retailing mavens (Arcadia, Bhs)	$9.1 [£4.85] BILLION
6. **Oleg Deripaska**, Russian business tycoon, controls Rusal, one of the world's largest aluminum producers	$8.2 [£4.375] BILLION
7. **Sir Richard Branson**, of Virgin Airlines, telecoms, music	$5.7 [£3] BILLION
8. **Kirsten and Jorn Rausing**, offspring of Tetra Pak founder	$4.9 [£2.58] BILLION
9. **David and Simon Reuben**, Bombay-born property developers, made fortune in Russia	$4.7 [£2.5] BILLION
10. **Spiro Latsis family**, son of Greek shipping tycoon, owns private bank, ships, property, oil refinery, aviation	$4.5 [£2.4] BILLION

NOTE: Queen Elizabeth II came in 180 on the UK rich list, with the *Sunday Times* estimating her wealth at $515 million (£270 million), including a $190 million personal investment portfolio.

**2005 ranking by the* Sunday Times *of London*

The Starbucks Timeline:
The Growth of an Empire

1971 First Starbucks store opens in Seattle's Pike Place Market.

1982 Howard Schultz joins Starbucks as director of retail operations.

1984 Starbucks opens coffee bar in downtown Seattle.

1987 Starbucks opens in Chicago and Vancouver. *Store total at end of year: **17**.*

1988 Starbucks mail-order catalog launched. *Store total at end of year: **33**.*

1989 Starbucks store opens in Portland, Oregon. *Store total at end of year: **55**.*

1990 *Store total at end of year: **84**.*

1991 Starbucks opens in Los Angeles and Sea-Tac Airport. *Store total at end of year: **116**.*

1992 Becomes publicly traded company under ticker symbol SBUX. Stores open in San Francisco, San Diego, and Denver. *Store total at end of year: **165**.*

1993 Stores open in Washington, D.C. *Store total at end of year: **272**.*

1994 Stores open in Minneapolis, Boston, New York, Atlanta, Dallas, and Houston. *Store total at end of year:* ***425***.

1995 Starts selling compact discs. Agrees to open cafés in Japan in joint venture with Japanese company SAZABY. New stores open in Philadelphia, Pittsburgh, Las Vegas, Cincinnati, Baltimore, San Antonio, and Austin, Texas. *Store total at end of year:* ***677***.

1996 Stores open in Rhode Island, Idaho, North Carolina, Arizona, Utah, and Ontario, Canada. *Store total at end of year:* ***1,015***.

1997 Stores open in Florida, Michigan, Wisconsin, and the Philippines. *Store total at end of year:* ***1,412***.

1998 Stores open in New Orleans, St. Louis, Kansas City (Missouri), Portland (Maine), Taiwan, Thailand, New Zealand, and Malaysia. *Store total at end of year:* ***1,886***.

1999 Stores open in China, Kuwait, Korea, and Lebanon. *Store total at end of year:* ***2,135***.

2000 Stores open in Dubai, Hong Kong, Shanghai, Qatar, Bahrain, Saudi Arabia, and Australia. *Store total at end of year:* ***3,501***.

2001 Opens 300th store in Japan, and introduces Starbucks to Switzerland, Israel, and Austria. *Store total at end of year:* ***4,709***.

(Continued on page 100)

(Continued from page 99)

2002	Stores open in Oman, Indonesia, Germany, Spain, Puerto Rico, Mexico, Greece, and Southern China. *Store total at end of year:* ***6,193***.
2003	Opens 1000th Asian Pacific store in Beijing, launches Starbucks in Turkey, Chile, and Peru. *Store total at end of year:* ***7,225***.
2004	Stores open in Paris. *Store total at end of year:* ***8,569***.
2005	A four-story store in Seoul, Korea—the largest store in the Starbucks system—closes after rent was raised 300 percent to $100,000 a month.

STARBUCKS WAS NAMED FOR THE FIRST MATE IN HERMAN MELVILLE'S NOVEL *MOBY DICK*.

. . . And You Thought Your Accountant's Fee Was High?

Here are the fees some U.S. companies paid for professional audit services for 2004:

Goldman Sachs	$36 million to PricewaterhouseCoopers
General Electric	$102.6 million to KPMG
3M	$13.2 million to PricewaterhouseCoopers
Apple Computer	$4.2 million to KPMG
IBM	$76.7 million to PricewaterhouseCoopers
Pfizer	$39.2 million to KPMG

TOP 20

Companies for New College Graduates

Number of 2005 graduates these companies were planning to hire:

1. Enterprise Rent-A-Car	7,000
2. PricewaterhouseCoopers	3,170
3. Ernst & Young	2,900
4. Lockheed Martin	2,863
5. KPMG	2,240
6. Sodexho	2,050
7. Fairfax County Public Schools	1,600
8. Accenture	1,540
9. Northrop Grumman	1,266
10. United States Customs & Border Protection	1,200
11. Target	1,127
12. U.S. Air Force	1,095
13. Raytheon	1,000
14. Microsoft	970
15. JPMorgan Chase	810
16. Procter & Gamble	569
17. Liberty Mutual	545
18. Grant Thornton	500
19. Bank of America	413
20. U.S. Air Force Personnel Center/DPKR	400

5 U.S. Stocks You Should Have Bought in 2000

Panera Bread (PNRA), based in Richmond Heights, Missouri, operates and franchises more than 700 bakery/cafés in 35 states under the names Panera and Saint Louis Bread Company.

$1,000 invested in Panera Bread shares on the first trading day of 2000 would have expanded to $14,588 by March 31, 2005.

William Lyon Homes (WLS), based in Newport Beach, California, builds single-family homes, primarily in California, Arizona, and Nevada.

$1,000 invested in William Lyon Homes stock at the start of 2000 would have grown to $13,945 by March 31, 2005.

Hansen Natural (HANS), based in Corona, California, makes a broad line of "alternative" sodas, juices, and teas.

$1,000 invested in Hansen shares on the first day of trading in 2000 would have grown to $13,902 by March 31, 2005.

Pediatrix Medical Group (PDX), based in Sunrise, Florida, staffs and manages more than 220 hospital-based intensive care units providing care for babies born prematurely or with medical complications.

$1,000 invested in Pediatrix shares at the start of 2000 would have grown to $9,799 by March 31, 2005.

DaVita (DVA), based in El Segundo, California, operates more than 650 dialysis centers for patients suffering from kidney failure.

$1,000 invested in DaVita shares on the first day of trading in 2000 would have been worth $9,387 by March 31, 2005.

5 U.S. Stocks You Should Have Avoided in 2000

Critical Path (CPTH), based in San Francisco, California, designs software enabling companies to deliver spam-free, virus-free messenger services.

$1,000 invested in Critical Path shares at the start of 2000 would have evaporated to $1.91 by March 31, 2005.

Ariba (ARBA), based in Sunnyvale, California, designs software to help companies manage their supply chains.

$1,000 invested in Ariba shares on the first trading day of 2000 declined to $14.58 by March 31, 2005.

Sycamore Networks (SCMR), based in Chelmsford, Massachusetts, makes optical switches and transmission equipment for Internet connections.

$1,000 invested in Sycamore shares at the start of 2000 would have declined to $34.68 by March 31, 2005.

DoubleClick (DCLK), based in New York City, is an online advertising agency.

$1,000 invested in DoubleClick shares on the first trading day of 2000 was worth $60.85 by March 31, 2005.

InfoSpace (INSP), based in Bellevue, Washington, is an online directory source (yellow pages, white pages, maps).

$1,000 invested in InfoSpace shares on the first trading day of 2000 zoomed down to $76.32 by March 31, 2005.

Note: Final return assumes that all dividends and distributions were reinvested in stock.

Top 50 Companies Recognized for Diversity

1. Altria
2. Turner Broadcasting System
3. Citigroup
4. PepsiCo
5. Abbott Laboratories
6. Coca-Cola
7. Xerox
8. Allstate Insurance
9. Verizon Communications
10. Kraft Foods
11. Ford Motor
12. Marriott International
13. KeyBank
14. Pepsi Bottling Group
15. SBC Communications
16. Sears, Roebuck
17. Health Care Service
18. Tribune
19. Pitney Bowes
20. HSBC North America
21. New York Life
22. American Express
23. General Mills
24. Merck
25. JPMorgan Chase
26. Bank of America
27. Procter & Gamble
28. Knight Ridder
29. Wal-Mart
30. IKON Office Solutions
31. Wachovia
32. Prudential Financial
33. Bausch & Lomb
34. Comerica Bank
35. Unilever Foods NA
36. MetLife
37. Sprint
38. SunTrust
39. Colgate-Palmolive
40. Wells Fargo
41. Staples
42. BellSouth
43. Visteon
44. Eastman Kodak
45. Cingular Wireless
46. Nielsen Media Research
47. Chubb
48. General Motors
49. MasterCard
50. SC Johnson

How to Deal with White-Collar Crime

In September 2004, the Chinese government executed four bank executives for fraud totaling $15 million. The two banks involved were state-owned entities. Wang Liming, an accounting officer at China Construction Bank, was put to death, along with an accomplice, Miao Ping, for stealing 20 million yuan (about $2.4 million) from the bank. Another employee at China Construction, Wang Xiag, was executed for stealing another 20 million yuan in an unrelated case. The fourth man executed was Liang Shihan, an official at Bank of China's branch in the southern city of Zhuhai. He was accused of stealing $10.3 million.

China executes more criminals than the rest of the world combined.

Meanwhile, in Japan . . .

Yasuo Hamanaka, a Japanese copper trader, was responsible for what is believed to have been the most costly white-collar crime in history. In 1997, Hamanaka pleaded guilty to forgery and fraud in illegal copper trading that cost his employer, Sumitomo, $2.6 billion over ten years. He was sentenced to eight years in prison by a Tokyo District Court Judge.

How did "Blue Chip" stocks get their name? The term was taken from the game of poker, where blue chips are more valuable than white or red chips.

All-Time Worldwide Box Office Rankings*

	BOX OFFICE
1. *Titanic* (1997)	$1,835,300,000
2. *The Lord of the Rings: The Return of the King* (2003)	$1,129,219,252
3. *Harry Potter and the Sorcerer's Stone* (2001)	$968,600,000
4. *Star Wars: Episode I— The Phantom Menace* (1999)	$922,379,000
5. *The Lord of the Rings: The Two Towers* (2002)	$921,600,000
6. *Jurassic Park* (1993)	$919,700,000
7. *Shrek 2* (2004)	$880,871,036
8. *Harry Potter and the Chamber of Secrets* (2002)	$866,300,000
9. *Finding Nemo* (2003)	$865,000,000
10. *The Lord of the Rings: The Fellowship of the Ring* (2001)	$860,700,000
11. *Independence Day* (1996)	$811,200,000
12. *Spider-Man* (2002)	$806,700,000
13. *Star Wars* (1977)	$797,900,000
14. *Harry Potter and the Prisoner of Azkaban* (2004)	$789,458,727
15. *Spider-Man 2* (2004)	$783,577,893
16. *The Lion King* (1994)	$783,400,000
17. *E.T. the Extra-Terrestrial* (1982)	$756,700,000
18. *The Matrix Reloaded* (2003)	$735,600,000

	BOX OFFICE
19. *Forrest Gump* (1994)	$679,400,000
20. *The Sixth Sense* (1999)	$661,500,000
21. *Pirates of the Caribbean: The Curse of the Black Pearl* (2003)	$653,200,000
22. *Star Wars: Episode II— Attack of the Clones* (2002)	$648,200,000
23. *The Incredibles* (2004)	$624,037,578
24. *The Lost World: Jurassic Park* (1997)	$614,300,000
25. *The Passion of the Christ* (2004)	$604,370,943
26. *Men in Black* (1997)	$587,200,000
27. *Star Wars: Episode VI— The Return of the Jedi* (1983)	$575,700,000
28. *Armageddon* (1998)	$554,600,000
29. *Mission: Impossible II* (2000)	$545,300,000
30. *Star Wars: Episode V— The Empire Strikes Back* (1980)	$533,800,000
31. *Home Alone* (1990)	$533,800,000
32. *Monsters, Inc.* (2001)	$528,900,000
33. *The Day After Tomorrow* (2004)	$527,939,919
34. *Ghost* (1990)	$517,600,000
35. *Terminator 2: Judgment Day* (1991)	$516,800,000
36. *Aladdin* (1992)	$501,900,000
37. *Indiana Jones and the Last Crusade* (1989)	$494,800,000
38. *Twister* (1996)	$494,700,000
39. *Toy Story 2* (1999)	$485,700,000
40. *Troy* (2004)	$481,228,348
41. *Saving Private Ryan* (1998)	$479,300,000
42. *Jaws* (1975)	$470,600,000

(Continued on page 108)

(Continued from page 107)

	BOX OFFICE
43. *Pretty Woman* (1990)	$463,400,000
44. *Bruce Almighty* (2003)	$458,900,000
45. *The Matrix* (1999)	$456,300,000
46. *Gladiator* (2000)	$456,200,000
47. *Shrek* (2001)	$455,100,000
48. *Mission: Impossible* (1996)	$452,500,000
49. *Pearl Harbor* (2001)	$450,400,000
50. *Ocean's Eleven* (2001)	$444,200,000
51. *The Last Samurai* (2003)	$435,400,000
52. *Tarzan* (1999)	$435,200,000
53. *Meet the Fockers* (2004)	$431,987,890
54. *Men in Black II* (2002)	$425,600,000
55. *Die Another Day* (2002)	$424,700,000
56. *Dances with Wolves* (1990)	$424,200,000
57. *Cast Away* (2000)	$424,000,000
58. *The Matrix Revolutions* (2003)	$424,000,000
59. *Mrs. Doubtfire* (1993)	$423,200,000
60. *The Mummy Returns* (2001)	$418,700,000
61. *Terminator 3: Rise of the Machines* (2003)	$418,200,000
62. *The Mummy* (1999)	$413,300,000
63. *Batman* (1989)	$413,200,000
64. *Rain Man* (1988)	$412,800,000
65. *The Bodyguard* (1992)	$410,900,000
66. *Signs* (2002)	$407,900,000
67. *X2* (2003)	$406,400,000
68. *Gone With the Wind* (1939)	$390,500,000
69. *Robin Hood: Prince of Thieves* (1991)	$390,500,000
70. *Raiders of the Lost Ark* (1981)	$383,900,000
71. *Grease* (1978)	$379,800,000

	BOX OFFICE
72. *Ice Age* (2002)	$378,300,000
73. *Beauty and the Beast* (1991)	$378,300,000
74. *Godzilla* (1998)	$375,800,000
75. *What Women Want* (2000)	$370,800,000
76. *The Fugitive* (1993)	$368,700,000
77. *True Lies* (1994)	$365,200,000
78. *Die Hard: With a Vengeance* (1995)	$365,000,000
79. *Notting Hill* (1999)	$363,000,000
80. *Jurassic Park III* (2001)	$362,900,000
81. *There's Something About Mary* (1998)	$360,000,000
82. *Planet of the Apes* (2001)	$358,900,000
83. *The Flintstones* (1994)	$358,500,000
84. *Toy Story* (1995)	$358,100,000
85. *Minority Report* (2002)	$358,000,000
86. *A Bug's Life* (1998)	$357,900,000
87. *The Exorcist* (1973)	$357,500,000
88. *My Big Fat Greek Wedding* (2002)	$356,500,000
89. *Basic Instinct* (1992)	$352,700,000
90. *The World Is Not Enough* (1999)	$352,000,000
91. *GoldenEye* (1995)	$351,500,000
92. *Ocean's Twelve* (2004)	$351,331,634
93. *Back to the Future* (1985)	$350,600,000
94. *Se7en* (1995)	$350,100,000
95. *Hannibal* (2001)	$349,200,000
96. *Who Framed Roger Rabbit* (1988)	$349,200,000
97. *Deep Impact* (1998)	$348,600,000
98. *Dinosaur* (2000)	$347,800,000
99. *Pocahontas* (1995)	$347,800,000
100. *Tomorrow Never Dies* (1997)	$346,600,000

**Data from IMDb.com*

PROFILE

Avon Products

NOT MANY PEOPLE may remember that Avon Products, the door-to-door seller of cosmetics and personal care products, once owned the upscale jeweler Tiffany. Looking to diversify, Avon bought Tiffany in 1979 for $105 million in stock. After five years, it decided that selling diamonds was not its forte, so it sold Tiffany to an investment group headed by William Chaney, who had been running the business for Avon. The sales price was $135 million, netting Avon a $30 million gain. But in 2005, Tiffany's market value was $4.6 billion.

The people who made the decisions to buy and sell Tiffany were all men. Although 99 percent of its sales representatives and 99.9 percent of its customers have always been women, for the first 100 years of its existence—Avon was founded in 1886—top management of the company was dominated by men. As recently as 1971, Avon had only one female vice president. It took 113 years for Avon to find a woman to head the company. Andrea Jung became CEO in 1999.

But now Avon has more women managers than any other Fortune 500 company. Half the members of its board of directors, a third of its senior management team, 75 percent of its district sales mangers, and 82 percent of its division managers are women.

Avon began expanding internationally in 1954, and now it derives more than 70 percent of its nearly $8 billion annual sales outside America. The door-to-door selling pioneered in the United States is used overseas, except in China, where Avon products are sold in some 6,000 boutiques. The reason: China has a ban on selling door to door. Avon has been lobbying to get that ban rescinded—and it has a perfect advocate in its CEO, who speaks fluent Mandarin Chinese. She appears to be succeeding—in April 2005 the Ministry of Commerce in China permitted Avon to test direct selling in Beijing, Tianjin, and Guandong Province.

THERE ARE WINERIES OPERATING IN ALL 50 OF THE UNITED STATES. CALIFORNIA HAS THE MOST, WITH MORE THAN 2,000, AND DELAWARE HAS THE FEWEST, WITH JUST ONE.

U.S. Credit Card Kings

Leading issuers of credit cards, based on outstanding credit balances at end of 2004

BANK	OUTSTANDING BALANCES
JPMorgan Chase	$134.7 billion
Citigroup	$115.9 billion
MBNA	$82.12 billion
American Express	$63.6 billion
Bank of America	$61.0 billion
Capital One	$53.0 billion
Morgan Stanley (Discover)	$45.6 billion
HSBC	$22.7 billion
Providian	$18.5 billion
Wells Fargo	$13.4 billion

Note: Bank of America took over MBNA in 2006, and Washington Mutual took over Providian.

In 2004, Ireland had the lowest unemployment of all countries in the European Union, at 4.5 percent. Poland had the highest unemployment, at 18.8 percent.

WHATEVER HAPPENED TO . . .

POLAROID

— FOUNDED 1937 —

The inventor of instant photography filed for bankruptcy in 2001. One Equity Partners, a unit of JPMorgan Chase, bought the company at bankruptcy auction, chopped costs, reduced employment to 2,850 (at one point Polaroid employed 12,000), and licensed the Polaroid name. A Minnesota licensee, the Petters Group, put the Polaroid name on Asian-made TVs and DVDs and sold them into Wal-Mart and Target stores. In 2005 Petters acquired Polaroid for $425 million.

IN THE IMMORTAL WORDS OF . . .

"Nivea is one of Germany's most precious jewels."

—Gerhard Schröder, chancellor of Germany. Schröder was referring to the skin cream made by the Hamburg company Beiersdorf, which, in 2003, beat back a takeover attempt by Procter & Gamble.

Toughest Business in the Big Apple

NEW YORK CITY HAS 18,000 RESTAURANTS.
1,000 NEW ONES OPEN EVERY YEAR.
FOUR OUT OF FIVE NEW RESTAURANTS GO OUT OF BUSINESS WITHIN FIVE YEARS.

10 Largest Privately Owned Companies in the United States

	2004 SALES	EMPLOYEES
1. Cargill (Minneapolis, Minnesota)	$66.7 billion	115,500
2. Koch Industries (Wichita, Kansas)	$60 billion	30,000
3. Mars (McLean, Virginia)	$19.1 billion	39,000
4. PricewaterhouseCoopers (New York, New York)	$18.7 billion	122,000
5. Publix Supermarkets (Lakeland, Florida)	$18.7 billion	128,000
6. Bechtel (San Fransisco, California)	$17.4 billion	40,000
7. Ernst & Young (New York, New York)	$16.9 billion	106,000
8. C&S Wholesale Grocers (Keene, New Hampshire)	$15.2 billion	15,000
9. SemGroup (Tulsa, Oklahoma)	$12.57 billion	103,453
10. Meijer (Grand Rapids, Michigan)	$12.5 billion	65,000

For as long as anyone can remember, the largest winery in the United States has been E. & J. Gallo, of Modesto, California. It ships 75 million cases a year under a variety of labels. You are drinking a Gallo product if you pour from any of these labels: Gallo, Gallo of Sonoma, Gossamer Bay, Livingston Cellars, Carlo Rossi, Peter Vella, Wild Vines, Barelli Creek, Frei Ranch, Laguna, Stefani, Two Rock, Turning Leaf, Redwood Creek, Indigo Hills, Tott's, Ballatore, André, or E&J brandies and liqueur.

Where Nike Gets Its Products

Oregon-based Nike, the world's largest sportswear company, takes in more than $12 billion a year, 61 percent coming from outside the United States and 53 percent from shoe sales. In addition to the Nike brand, the company owns Cole Haan, g Series, Bragano, Bauer (hockey equipment), Hurley (apparel for surfers and skateboarders), Converse, Starter, and Asphalt. The company has 24,300 employees, about half of which are in the United States. Virtually all the shoes, apparel, and sports equipment sold by Nike are made by contract factories.

The Nike product comes from 703 factories located in 52 countries; some 625,000 employees work in those factories. About 200,000 work in 124 factories in China. Another 84,000 work in 34 plants in Vietnam. The United States has 49 plants. Other factory locations are listed on the opposite page.

Responding to protests, Nike now has a comprehensive monitoring system to ensure that workers in these plants, even though they are not direct employees of Nike, are not being abused. The system calls for training and education, on-the-spot audits, and termination of contracts if standards are not met. Nike has more than 90 employees involved in this monitoring program.

Countries with Nike Factories

Thailand:	73
Indonesia:	39
Korea:	35
Malaysia:	33
Turkey:	26
Sri Lanka:	25
Japan:	22
Mexico:	20
Portugal:	20
Taiwan:	19
India:	18
Brazil:	18
Italy:	13
Canada:	10
Australia:	9
Tunisia:	9
Hong Kong:	9
Honduras:	8
Bulgaria:	8
South Africa:	7
Argentina:	7
El Salvador:	6
Israel:	6
United Kingdom:	5
Bangladesh:	5
Spain:	5
Morocco:	4
Philippines:	4
Egypt:	4
Pakistan:	3
Macau:	3
Jordan:	3
Chile:	2
Colombia:	2
Singapore:	2
Albania:	1
Belgium:	1
Cambodia:	1
Dominican Republic:	1
Ecuador:	1
Fiji:	1
Greece:	1
Guatemala:	1
Macedonia:	1
Moldova:	1
Lithuania:	1
New Zealand:	1
Peru:	1
Switzerland:	1

WHATEVER HAPPENED TO . . .

BORDEN

— Founded 1857—

Once the world's largest food company—Gail Borden invented condensed milk, and the company was the first to put fresh milk into bottles—Borden lost its way in the 1980s, selling and buying companies at a rapid clip. Meanwhile, it was making more money in chemicals than in foods. In 1995 the investment firm Kohlberg, Kravis, Roberts acquired Borden in a leveraged buyout and then sold off the food businesses, including Cracker Jack, Creamette and Prince pastas, Snow's Clam Chowder, ReaLemon, and Wise's Cheez Doodles. In 2004 the investment firm Apollo Management took control of Borden Chemical.

Millions of Millionaires

As of 2004, 8.3 million people in the world have $1 million to spend, invest, or save, according to the Capgemini/Merrill Lynch World Wealth Report 2005. This assessment excludes the value of homes and pensions. The number of people in this class went up by 600,000 in 2004. Collectively, this group holds $30.8 trillion in assets. Geographically, they break down as follows:

North America: 2.7 million

Europe: 2.6 million

Asia-Pacific: 2.3 million

Latin America: 300,000

Middle East: 300,000

Africa: 100,000

FRATRICIDE

The Dassler Brothers

Adolf Dassler

ADIDAS ATHLETIC SHOES originated in the tiny Bavarian milltown of Herzogenaurach, near Nurnberg. Before World War II, two brothers, Adolf and Rudolf Dassler, sons of a poor laundress, started a factory to make house slippers. They soon branched out into track shoes and soccer boots. But the Dassler brothers had a violent falling out, and they went their separate ways after the war. Rudolf Dassler set up a rival athletic shoe company, marketing under the brand Puma.

Adidas and Puma now go head-to-head in this market. Both companies are still headquartered in Herzogenaurach.

TSINGTAO is China's largest brewer, operating 50 breweries in 18 provinces and cities. It holds 13 percent of the Chinese beer market. And like a lot of major companies in China, the government holds a major stake: 30 percent.

But the second largest shareholder is none other than Anheuser-Busch of St. Louis, Missouri, brewer of Budweiser and Bud Light. In 2005, the American company boosted its holdings in Tsingtao to 27 percent of the outstanding shares. The purchase followed Anheuser-Busch's 2004 acquisition of the number four brewer in China, Harbin—just in time for the 2008 Olympic Games in Beijing.

TOP 13
Pharmaceutical Companies

	2004 SALES
1. Pfizer (U.S.)	$51.1 billion
2. GlaxoSmithKline (UK)	$32.8 billion
3. Sanofi-Aventis (France)	$27.4 billion
4. Johnson & Johnson (U.S.)	$24.7 billion
5. Merck (U.S.)	$23.9 billion
6. Novartis (Switzerland)	$22.9 billion
7. Roche (Switzerland)	$17.8 billion
8. Bristol-Myers Squibb (U.S.)	$15.6 billion
9. Wyeth Laboratories (U.S.)	$14.3 billion
10. Abbott Laboratories (U.S.)	$14.3 billion
11. Eli Lilly (U.S.)	$12.7 billion
12. Schering-Plough (U.S.)	$6.9 billion
13. Bayer (Germany)	$6.4 billion

WHATEVER HAPPENED TO . . .

FIRESTONE

— FOUNDED 1900 —

The tire company involved in multiple lawsuits and recalls was sold in 1988 to Japan's Bridgestone, which has moved the headquarters from Akron, Ohio, to Nashville, Tennessee.

World's Largest Cosmetics Company

To find the world's number one cosmetics producer, go to the Paris suburb of Clichy, headquarters of L'Oreal. With a galaxy of brands sold in more than 150 countries, L'Oreal has distanced itself from rivals. Its revenues in 2004 totaled $18.8 billion, more than double those of Avon Products, triple Estée Lauder's, and 14 times Revlon's. L'Oreal's brand lineup looks like this: L'Oreal, Redken, Matrix, Garnier, Maybelline, SoftSheen/Carson, Lancome, Biotherm, Helena Rubenstein, Giorgio Armani, Ralph Lauren, Cacharel, Kiehl's, Shu Uemura, Vichy, La Roche-Posay. For 17 years, from 1988 to 2005, L'Oreal was run by a Welshman, Lindsay Owen-Jones.

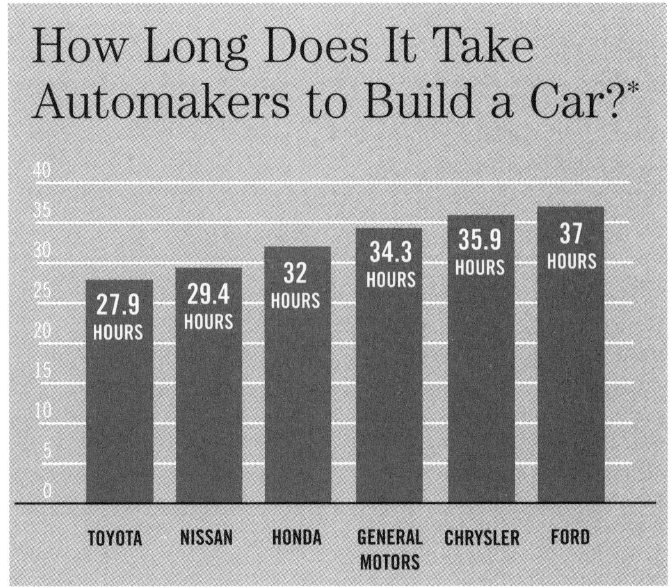

**Based on production in North American plants*

World's Largest Steel Company: Mittal

BETHLEHEM STEEL, LTV Steel, Inland Steel, Weirton Steel, Acme Steel, Georgetown Steel: Once pillars of the American steel industry, now they are subsumed in a global company. Mittal Steel, created by Indian-born Lakshmi Mittal, has operations in 14 countries on four continents. The company has placed its headquarters in the Dutch city of Rotterdam, but Lakshmi Mittal makes his home in the United Kingdom, where he was ranked by the *Sunday Times* in 2005 as the richest person in the country, with wealth estimated at £14.8 billion. Mittal Steel shares are listed on the New York and Eurotext Amsterdam stock exchanges, trading under the symbol MT.

Mittal Steel vaulted into first place in the world steel industry on April 13, 2005, with the acquisition of Richfield, Ohio, based International Steel Group (ISG), a collection of bankrupt steel companies assembled by the New York buyout firm W.L. Ross & Co. The purchase price, in cash and stock, was $4.5 billion. Mittal's American holdings now include four of the five steel mills on the Great Lakes, the Sparrows Point plant on Chesapeake Bay near Baltimore, iron ore mines near Virginia and Minnesota, and a bunch of mills and plants in Ohio, Pennsylvania, New York, and West Virginia.

Lakshmi Mittal

Mittal's lavish spending has been fodder for the London tabloids. He bought a $127 million mansion in London, and in 2004 he repeatedly spent $60 million to stage his daughter's wedding at a French chateau and the Versailles Palace. Mittal's son, Aditya, is president of Mittal Steel.

In a weird coincidence, as Mittal Steel rose to global dominance, on April 13, 2005, the largest industrial union in the United States was also formed. While shareholders of Mittal and ISG were meeting in Rotterdam and New York to seal their deal, labor leaders were meeting in Las Vegas to seal their deal, merging the United Steelworkers of America with the Paper, Allied-Industrial, Chemical, and Energy Workers International Union (PACE). The result is a union whose formal title is United Steel, Paper and Forestry, Rubber, Manufacturing, Energy, Allied Industrial and Service Workers International Union. Recognizing that this name is a bit of a mouthful, the labor guys call their union United Steelworkers, or USW for short.

The old United Steelworkers represented 650,000 workers across the United States. They have lost 100,000 members since 2000, but PACE represented 250,000 workers, which makes the new USW the largest industrial union in the country, topping the United Auto Workers.

Good luck negotiating with Lakshmi Mittal!

Location of Factories Producing Clothes for the Gap*

Southeast Asia	**671**
Indian Subcontinent	**592**
Greater China	**464**
Mexico, Central America, and the Caribbean	**298**
Europe	**277**
North Asia	**200**
United States and Canada	**188**
Sub-Saharan Africa	**118**
North Africa and Middle East	**91**
South America	**68**
Persian Gulf	**42**

**Includes Old Navy and Banana Republic stores*

5 European Stocks You Should Have Bought in 2000

Wallenstam (WALL-B), based in Goteborg, Sweden, is a real estate operator whose rental portfolio includes 10,000 residential apartments, 2,000 commercial properties, and 6,000 parking spaces in Sweden.

€1,000 invested in Wallenstam at the start of 2000 grew to €8,515 by March 31, 2005.

Lisbon-based **Sopol** (SPO) builds and maintains highways, roads, and industrial structures in Portugal.

€1,000 invested in Sopol shares at the end of 1999 would have been worth €8,274 by March 31, 2005.

Stockholm-based **Elekta** (EKTA-B) supplies systems and clinical procedures for treatment of severe diseases. Products include Leksell Gamma Knife, Neuromag Vectorview, and Brain Atlas.

€1,000 invested in Elekta shares at the start of 2000 would have grown to €8,197 by March 31, 2005.

Groupe Fructa Partner (5311), based in Villefranche Sur Saone, wholesales food and beverages to 5,820 retail outlets.

€1,000 invested in Fructa Partner at the start of 2000 increased in value to €8,042 by March 31, 2005.

Paris-based **Audika** (6375) makes hearing aids.

€1,000 invested in Audika shares at the start of 2000 grew to €8,041 by March 31, 2005.

5 European Stocks You Should Have Avoided in 2000

London-based **Earthport** (018570) sets up secure payment systems for companies.

€1,000 invested in Earthport shares at the start of 2000 would have evaporated to €0.007 by March 31, 2005.

Baeurer (BEU), based in Donaueschingen, Germany, designs software applications to help small- and medium-sized companies run their businesses better.

€1,000 invested in Baeurer shares at the start of 2000 would have plunged to €0.73 by March 31, 2005.

KPNQwest (KQIP), based in Hoofddorp, Netherlands, owns and operates EuroRings, a 15-country fiber-optic system to provide companies with networking solutions and Internet hosting services.

€1,000 invested in KQIP shares at the end of 1999 would have eroded to €0.76 by March 31, 2005.

Oslo-based **Petrolia Drilling** (PDR) operates oil drilling rigs in the North Sea.

€1,000 invested in Petrolia Drilling shares at the start of 2000 would have declined to €0.96 by March 31, 2005.

Pan Fish (PAN), based in Stavanger, Norway, farms, processes, and distributes salmon, trout, and other fish products.

€1,000 invested in Pan Fish shares at the end of 1999 would have declined to €1.07 by March 31, 2005.

Note: Final return assumes that all dividends and distributions were reinvested in stock.

PROFILE

Clear Channel Communications

Based in San Antonio, Texas, Clear Channel Communications went on a tear after 1996 when the new Telecommunications Act eased restrictions on the number of radio stations one company can own. Prior to 1996, a company could own no more than two stations in one market and no more than two dozen nationally.

Result: Clear Channel now owns 1,270 radio stations in the United States.

A STATE-BY-STATE RUNDOWN

ALABAMA Birmingham: WENN-FM, WERC-FM, WMJJ-FM, WDXB-FM, WQEN-FM Gadsen: WAAX-FM, WGMZ-FM Huntsville: WBHP-AM, WDRM-FM, WHOS-AM, WTAK-FM, WWXQ-FM, WXQW-FM Mobile: WDWG-FM, WKSJ-AM, WMXC-FM, WNTM-AM, WRKH-FM Montgomery: WMCZ-FM, WQLD-FM, WZHT-FM Tuscaloosa: WACT-AM, WRTR-FM, WTXT-FM, WZBQ-FM **ALASKA** Anchorage: KASH-FM, KBFX-FM, KENI-AM, KGOT-FM, KTZN-AM, KYMG-FM Fairbanks: KAKQ-FM, KIAK-AM/FM, KKED-FM **ARIZONA** Chinle: KFXR-FM Phoenix: KESZ-FM, KMXP-FM, KNIX-FM, KZZP-FM, KFYI-FM, KGME-FM, KOY-AM, KYOT-FM Tuba City: KAXB-FM Tuscon: KCEE-AM, KNST-AM, KRQQ-FM, KWFM-FM Yuma: KBLU-AM, KTTI-FM, FKYJT-FM **ARKANSAS** Little Rock: KDDK-FM, FMJX-FM, KOLL-FM, KQAR-FM, KSSN-FM Fayetteville: KEZA-FM, FJEM-FM, KKIX-FM, KMXF-FM Ft. Smith: KMAG-FM, KWHN-AM, KZBB-FM, KKBD-FM **CALIFORNIA** Anaheim: KEZY-AM Chico: KEWE-FM, KHHZ-FM, KHSL-FM, KPAY-AM Ellwood: KSPE-FM Lancaster: KAVL-AM/FM, KAVS-FM, KYHT-FM Los Angeles: KACD-FM, KAVL-AM, KAVS-FM, KIIS-FM, KXTA-AM, KOST-AM, KFI-AM, KYSR-FM, KBIG-FM, KCMG-FM, KLAC-AM Monterey: KDON-AM/FM, KOCN-FM, KRQC-FM, KTOM-AM/FM San Benardino: KCKC-AM San Diego: KGB-FM, KHTS-FM, KIOZ-FM, KJQY-FM, KMSX-FM, KOGO-AM, KPOP-AM, XHRM-FM, XTRA-AM San Francisco: KABL-AM, KIOI-FM, KISQ-FM, KKSF-FM, FMEL-FM, KNEW-FM, KYLD-FM San Jose: KCNL-FM, KFJO-FM, KLDZ-FM, KSJO-FM, KUFX-FM San Luis Obispo: KVEC-AM Santa Barbara: KIST-AM, KSBL-FM, KTMS-AM, KTYD-FM, KXXT-AM Santa Clarita: KBET-AM Thousand Oaks: KLYF-AM Victorville: KATJ-FM, KZXY-AM, KIXA-FM, KROY-AM, KIXW-AM Walnut Creek: KFJO-FM Yermo: KYHT-FM **COLORADO** Cortez: KISZ-FM Denver: KBCO-FM,

KBPI-FM, KHIH-FM, KHOW-AM, KOA-AM, KRFZ-FM, KTCL-FM, KTLK-AM Durango: KPTE-FM, KDGO-FM Fort Collins: KCOL-AM, KGLI-FM, KIIX-AM, KPAW-FM Vail: KSKE-FM **CONNECTICUT** New Haven: WAVZ-FM, WELI-AM, WKCI-FM **DELAWARE** Wilmington: WDOV-AM, WDSD-FM, WJBR-AM, WRDX-FM **FLORIDA** Daytona Beach: WGNE-FM Florida Keys: WAIL-FM, WAVK-FM, WCTH-FM, WEOW-FM, WFKZ-FM, WKEZ-AM/FM, WRWF-AM Ft. Myers/Naples: WCKT-FM, WOLZ-FM, WQNU-FM, WOST-FM Jacksonville: WHSJ-FM, WJBT-FM, WJGR-AM, WNZS-AM, WPLA-FM, WQIK-FM, WROO-FM, WSOL-FM, WZNZ-AM Melbourne: WBVD-FM, WLRQ-FM, WMMB-AM, WMMV-AM Miami/Ft. Lauderdale: WBGG-FM, WHYI-FM, WINZ-AM, WIOD-AM, WLVE-FM, WMGE-AM, WZTA-FM Orlando: WJRR-FM, WMGF-FM, WQTM-AM, WSHE-FM, WTKS-FM, WWNZ-AM Panama City: WDIZ-AM, WFSY-FM, WPAP-FM, WPBH-FM, WPPT-FM Pensacola: WTKX-FM Rock Punta Gorda: WCCF-AM, WCVU-FM, WIKX-FM, WKII-AM Sarasota: WAMR-AM, WCTQ-FM, WDDV-FM, WSPB-AM, WSRZ-FM, WYNF-FM Tallahasee: WTLY-FM, WNLS-AM, WOKI-FM, WINT-FM, WXSR-FM Tampa/St. Petersburg: WMTX-FM, WDAE-AM, WFLA-AM, WFLZ-FM, WHNZ-AM, WSSR-FM, WTBT-FM, WXTB-FM West Palm Beach: WBZT-AM, WIRA-AM, WINO-AM, WJNX-AM, WKGR-FM, WLDI-FM, WOLL-FM, WWLV-FM **GEORGIA** Atlanta: WCOH-AM, WGSE-AM, WGST-AM/FM, WKLS-FM, WMAX-FM, WMKJ-FM, WPCH-FM Helen: WHEL-FM Hogansville: WMXY-AM, WZLG-FM **HAWAII** Honolulu: KSSK-AM/FM, KDNN-FM, KIKI-FM, KUCD-FM, KHVH-AM, KHBZ-AM **IDAHO** Boise: KARO-FM, KCIX-FM, FFXD-AM, KIDO-AM, KLTB-FM, KXLT-FM Idaho Falls: KID-AM/FM Pocatello: KLLP-FM, KPKY-FM, KWIK-AM Twin Falls: KEZJ-FM, KLIX-AM/FM **ILLINOIS** Carbondale: WDDD-FM, WFRX-AM, WVZA-FM Chicago: WGCI-AM/FM, WKSC-FM, WLIT-FM, WNUA-FM, WVAZ-FM **INDIANA** Indianapolis: WFBQ-FM, WNDE-AM, WRZX-FM **IOWA** Burlington: KBUR-AM, KGRS-FM Cedar Rapids: WMT-AM/FM Davenport: KUUL-FM, KMXG-FM, KCQQ-FM, WLLR-AM/FM, WOC-AM Des Moines: WHO-AM, KKDM-FM, KLYF-FM, KMXD-FM, KCCQ-FM, KASI-AM Fort Dodge: KKEZ-FM, KWMT-AM Fort Madison: KBKB-AM/FM Iowa City: KKRQ-FM, KXIC-AM **KENTUCKY** Lexington: WBUL-FM, WKQQ-FM, WLAP-AM, WLKT-FM, WMXL-FM, WTKT-AM Louisville: WHAS-AM, WAMZ-FM, WQMF-FM, WTFX-FM, WWKY-AM, WKJK-AM, WYBL-FM, WZTR-FM Midway: WBTF-FM **LOUISIANA** New Orleans: KFXN-FM, WRNO-FM, WODT-AM/FM, WQUE-FM, WNOE-FM, WYLD-AM. Shreveport: KEEL-AM, KITT-FM, KRUF-FM, KVKI-FM, KWKH-AM **MAINE** Bangor: WGUY-FM, WVOM-FM, WBYA-FM, WBFB-FM, WKSQ-FM, WLKE-FM **MARYLAND** Baltimore: WCAO-AM, WOCT-FM, WPOC-FM Ocean City: WLVW-FM, WQHQ-FM, WTGM-AM, WAWR-AM, WSBY-FM, WWFG-FM, WLBW-FM, WOSC-FM **MASSACHUSETTS** Boston: WJMN-FM, WKOX-AM, WXKS-AM/FM Worcester: WSRS-FM, WTAG-AM Springfield: WHYN-AM/FM, WNNZ-AM **MICHIGAN** Ann Arbor: WIBQ-FM, WQKL-FM, WTKA-AM, WYBN-FM Detroit: WDFN-AM, WJLB-FM, WKQI-FM, WLLC-FM, WMXD-FM, WNIC-FM, WXDX-AM Grand Rapids: WBCT-AM, WCUZ-FM, WOOD-AM/FM, WTKG-AM, WVTI-FM, WSNX-FM **MINNESOTA** Twin Cities: KDWB-FM, KEEY-FM, KFAN-AM, KFXN-AM, KQQL-FM, KTCZ-FM, WLOL-FM **MISSISSIPPI** Jackson: WJMI-FM, WFXI-AM/FM, WOAD-AM, WYJS-FM **MISSOURI** St. Louis: KATZ-AM/FM, KLOU-FM, KMJM-FM, KSD-FM, KSLZ-FM **NEVADA** Las Vegas: KFMS-FM, KQOL-FM, KSNE-FM, KWNR-FM **NEW MEXICO** Albuquerque: KZRR-FM, KPEK-FM, KTEG-FM, KLSK-FM, KSYU-FM Farmington: KRWN-FM, KENN-AM, KNNT-AM Gallup: KGLX-FM, KFMQ-FM Las Vegas:

(Continued on page 126)

(Continued from page 125)

KBAC-FM Thoreau: KXTC-FM White Rock: KSFQ-FM **NEW YORK** Albany: WGY-AM, WHRL-FM, WKKF-FM, WOFX-AM, WPYX-FM, WRVE-FM, WTRY-FM Binghamton: WBBI-FM, WENE-AM, WINR-AM, WKGB-FM, WMRV-FM, WMXW-FM Nassau/Suffolk: WALK-AM/FM New York City: WAXQ-FM, WHTZ-FM, WKTU-FM, WLTW-FM, WTGM-FM Poughkeepsie: WRWD-FM, WBWZ-FM, WBPM-FM, WGHQ-AM Rochester: WHAM-AM, WHTK-AM, WKGS-FM, WLCL-FM, WMAX-FM, WNVE-FM, WVOR-FM Syracuse: WBBS-FM, WHEN-AM, WSRY-AM, WHHT-FM, WYYY-FM Utica: WADR-AM, WOUR-FM, WRFM-FM, WRNY-AM, WSKS-FM, WUTQ-AM **NORTH CAROLINA** Greensboro: WSJS-AM, WSML-AM, WTQR-FM, WXRA-FM Raleigh: WDUR-AM, WFXC-FM, WFXK-FM, WNNL-FM, WQOK-FM **NORTH DAKOTA** Bismarck: KFYR-AM, KYYY-FM Dickinson: KLTC-AM, KCAD-FM, KZRX-FM Fargo: FFGO-AM/FM, WDAY-FM, KVOX-AM, KULW-FM, KRVI-FM Minot: KIZZ-FM, KZPR-FM, KRRZ-FM **OHIO** Akron: WKDD-FM, WTOU-AM Chillicothe: WBEX-AM, WCHI-AM, WFCB-FM, WKKJ-FM Cincinnati: WCKY-AM, WEBN-FM, WKFS-FM, WKRC-AM, WLW-AM, WOFX-FM, WSAI-AM, WVMX-FM Cleveland: WGAR-FM, WMJI-FM, WMMS-FM, WMVX-FM, WTAM-AM Clyde: WMJK Columbus: WCOL-FM, WFII-AM, WNCI-FM, WTVN-AM, WZAZ-FM Dayton: WBTT-FM, WLQT-FM, WMMX-FM, WONE-AM, WTUE-FM, WXEG-FM Defiance: WDFM-FM, WZOM-FM, WONW-AM Findlay: WCKY-FM, WIMJ-FM, WQTL-FM Lima: WBUK-FM, WIMA-AM, WIMT-FM, WMLX-FM Lorain: WZLE-FM Mansfield: WYHT-FM, WSWR-FM, WMAN-AM Marion: WDIF-FM, WMRN-AM/FM Napoleon: WNDH-FM Sandusky: WMJF-FM, WLEC-AM, WCPZ-FM Springfield: WIZE-AM Tiffin: WCKY-FM, WTTE-AM Toledo: WCWA-AM, WIOT-FM, WRVF-FAM, WSPD-AM, WVKS-FM Washington Court House: WCHO-AM/FM Youngstown: WBTJ-FM, WKBN-AM, WNCD-FM, WNIO-AM **OKLAHOMA** Guymon: KGYN-AM Oklahoma City: KBEC-AM, KJYA-FM, KQSR-FM, KTOK-AM, KTST-FM, KXXY-FM, WKY-AM Tulsa: KAKC-AM, KMOD-FM, KMRX-FM, KOAS-FM, KQLL-AM, KIZS-FM **OREGON** Albany: KLOO-AM, KRKT-AM Corvallis: KEJO-AM, KFLY-FM, KLOO-AM/FM Medford: KKJJ-FM, KLDZ-FM, KMED-AM, KRWQ-FM, KZZE-FM Portland: KTLK-AM, KEX-AM, KKCW-FM, KKRZ-FM, KRVO-FM **PENNSYLVANIA** Allentown: WAEM-AM/FM, WKAP-AM, WZZO-FM Harrisburg: WHP-AM, WKBO-AM, WRBT-FM, WRVV-FM, WWKL-AM Johnstown: WMTZ-FM, WNTJ-AM Lancaster/Harrisburg: WLAN-AM/FM New Castle: WBZY-AM, WKST-AM/FM Philadelphia: WDAS-AM/FM, WIOQ-FM, WJJZ-FM, WLCE-FM, WUSL-FM Pittsburgh: WBGG-AM, WDVE-FM, WJJJ-FM, WKST-FM, WWSW-FM, WXDX-FM Reading: WRAW-AM, WRFY-FM, WREX-FM Williamsport: WKSB-FM, WMYL-FM, WRAK-AM, WRKK-AM **RHODE ISLAND** Providence: WWBB-FM, WWRX-FM **SOUTH CAROLINA** Charleston: WLAC-FM, WEZL-FM, WRFQ-FM, WSCC-AM, WXYL-FM Columbia: WCOS-AM/FM, WLTY-FM, WNOK-FM, WSCQ-FM, WVOC-AM Greenville: WESC-AM, WJMZ-FM, WPTP-FM **SOUTH DAKOTA** Aberdeen: KKAA-AM, KQAA-FM, KSDN-AM/FM, KBFO-FM **TENNESSEE** Chattanooga: WUSY-FM, WUUS-AM, WRXR-FM, WLOV-FM, WKXJ-FM Cookeville: WGIC-FM, WGSQ-FM, WHUB-AM, WPTN-AM Memphis: KJMS-FM, KWAM-AM, WDIA-AM, WEGR-FM, WHRK-FM, WOTO-FM, WREC-AM, WYLT-FM Nashville: WLAC-AM, WNRQ-FM, WRVW-FM, WSIX-FM, WZTO-FM St. Joseph: WJOR-FM **TEXAS** Austin: KHKI-FM, KPEZ-FM Beaumont: KOIC-FM, KKMY-FM, KYKR-FM, KLVI-AM Dallas: KDMX-FM, KEGL-FM, KHEY-AM/FM, KPRR-FM, KTSM-AM/FM, XHEPR-FM Houston: JAMZ, KBXX-FM, KHMX-FM, KKTL-FM, KPRC-AM, KTBZ-FM McAllen: KTEX-FM,

KBFM-FM San Antonio: KAJA-FM, KQXT-FM, KSJL-FM, KTKR-AM, KXXM-FM, WOAI-AM Waco: KBGO-FM, KBRQ-FM, KWTX-AM/FM, WACO-FM Wichita Falls: WKNIN-FM, KWFS-AM/FM, KTLT-FM **UTAH** Salt Lake City: KALL-AM, KKAT-FM, KNRS-AM, KODJ-FM, KURR-FM, KWLW-AM, KZHT-FM **VERMONT** Burlington: WCPV-FM, WEAV-AM, WEZF-FM, WJVT-FM, WXZO-FM Randolph: WCVR-FM, WSYB-AM, WWWT-AM, WZRT-FM **VIRGINIA** Charlottesville: WCYK-FM, WVAO-FM, WUMX-FM Norfolk: WJCD-FM, WOWI-FM, WSVY-AM/FM Richmond: WBTJ-FM, WRNL-AM, WRVA-AM, WRVQ-FM, WRXL-FM, WTVR-FM **WASHINGTON** Centralia: KELA-AM, KMNT-FM Seattle: KFNK-FM, KHHO-AM, KJT-AM/FM, KUBE-FM Vancouver: KKLQ-FM **WASHINGTON, D.C.** WASH-FM, WBIG-FM, WIHT-FM, WMZQ-FM, WTEM-AM, WTNT-AM, WWDC-FM, WWRC-AM **WEST VIRGINIA** Huntington: WAMX-FM, WBKS-FM, WBVB-FM, WHRD-AM, WIRO-AM, WKEE-FM, WTCR-AM/FM, WVHU-AM Wheeling: WBBD-AM, WEEL-FM, WEGW-FM, WKWK-FM, WOVK-FM, WVKF-FM, WWVA-AM **WISCONSIN** Eau Claire: WATQ-FM, WBIZ-AM/FM, WMEQ-AM/FM, WQRB-FM Madison: WMAD-FM, WCJZ-FM, WIBA-AM/FM, WZEE-FM, WTSO-AM Milwaukee: WKKV-FM, WMIL-FM, WOKY-AM, WRIT-FM **WYOMING** Casper: KRVK-FM, KTRS-FM, KWYY-FM, KMGW-FM, KTWO-AM, KKTL-AM Cheyenne: KGAB-AM, KIGN-GM, KMUS-FM, KOLS-FM

ON TOP OF THAT, CLEAR CHANNEL OWNS 39 TELEVISION STATIONS

WXXA-TV, Albany, New York (Fox affiliate) **KGET-TV**, Bakersfield, California (NBC affiliate) **KVOS-TV**, Bellingham, Washington (independent) **WIVT-TV**, Binghamton, New York (ABC affiliate) **WKRC-TV**, Cincinnati, Ohio (CBS affiliate) **WETM-TV**, Elmira, New York (NBC affiliate) **KMTR-TV**, Springfield, Oregon (NBC affiliate) **KMTX-TV**, Roseburg, Oregon (NBC affiliate) **KTMZ-TV**, Coos Bay, Oregon (NBC affiliate) **KVIQ-TV**, Eureka, California (CBS affiliate) **KTVF-TV**, Fairbanks, Alaska (NBC affiliate) **KPGE-TV**, Fresno, California (CBS affiliate) **WHP-TV**, Harrisburg, Pennsylvania (UPN affiliate) **WLYH-TV**, Harrisburg, Pennsylvania (UPN affiliate) **WJKT-TV**, Jackson, Tennessee (UPN affiliate) **WAWS-TV**, Jacksonville, Florida (Fox affiliate) **WTEV-TV**, Jacksonville, Florida (CBS affiliate) **KASN-TV**, Little Rock, Arkansas (UPN affiliate) **KLRT-TV**, Little Rock, Arkansas (Fox affiliate) **WLMT-TV**, Memphis, Tennessee (UPN affiliate) **WPTY-TV**, Memphis, Tennesse (ABC affiliate) **WJTC-TV**, Mobile, Alabama, (UPN affiliate) **WPMI-TV**, Mobile, Alabama (NBC affiliate) **KCBA-TV**, Monterey/Salinas, California (Fox affiliate) **KION-TV**, Monterey/Salinas, California (CBS affiliate) **WORK-TV**, Rochester, New York, (ABC affiliate) **KTVX-TV**, Salt Lake City, Utah (ABC affiliate) **WOAI-TV**, San Antonio, Texas (NBC affiliate) **KPXL-TV**, San Antonio, Texas (PAX affiliate) **KCOY-TV**, Santa Maria, California (CBS affiliate) **KFTY-TV**, Santa Rosa, California (independent) **WIXT-TV**, Syracuse, New York (ABC affiliate) **KOKI-TV**, Tulsa, Oklahoma (Fox affiliate) **KTFO-TV**, Tulsa, Oklahoma (UPN affiliate) **WUTR-TV**, Utica, New York (ABC affiliate) **WWTI-TV**, Watertown, New York (ABC affiliate) **KAAS-TV**, Wichita, Kansas (Fox affiliate) **KSAS-TV**, Wichita, Kansas (Fox affiliate) **KSCC-TV**, Wichita, Kansas (UPN affiliate)

WHEN THE 1980S BEGAN, THE UNITED STATES HAD SIX MAJOR TIRE PRODUCERS: GOODYEAR, FIRESTONE, UNIROYAL, GOODRICH, GENERAL, AND ARMSTRONG. ALL EXCEPT ONE, GOODYEAR, HAVE SINCE BEEN TAKEN OVER BY FOREIGN FIRMS.

Odd Couplings

American International Group, the world's largest insurance company, owns the Stowe, Vermont, ski resort.

General Electric owns NBC.

Fortune Brands owns Jim Beam bourbon, Titleist golf balls, Absolut Vodka, Courvoisier brandy, Moen Faucets, Sauza tequila, Master Lock padlocks, and Canadian Club whisky.

Rupert Murdoch's **News Corp.** owns the *Times* Literary Supplement, *News of the World*, the Fox television network, HarperCollins publishers, and the *New York Post*.

Mars, leading candy company (M&Ms, Snickers, Mars), owns Uncle Ben's rice and pet food brands Whiskas and Pedigree.

Japan's **Yamaha**, a leading supplier of pianos, guitars, and other musical instruments, also makes golf clubs, industrial robots, kitchen and bathroom units, stereo equipment, and semiconductors, and operates golf courses, ski resorts, and hotels.

Who Buys the Most Insurance

ANNUAL INSURANCE PREMIUMS PER CAPITA

Switzerland	$5,000
United Kingdom	$3,900
Japan	$3,400
United States	$3,300
Ireland	$2,700
Netherlands	$2,400
Denmark	$2,400
Finland	$2,200
France	$2,000
Belgium	$1,500

TOTAL INSURANCE PREMIUM VOLUME

United States	$1 trillion
Japan	$479 billion
United Kingdom	$250 billion
Germany	$170 billion
France	$164 billion

France is one of the best markets for McDonald's, where its restaurants rang up sales of $2.8 billion in 2004.

PROFILE

Pemex

PEMEX—SHORT FOR PETRÓLEOS MEXICANOS—is the world's third largest producer of crude oil. With annual revenues of $69 billion, it is easily the highest earning company not only in Mexico but in all of Latin America. It's also one of the largest employers in Latin America, with 142,000 people on its payroll. However, according to David Luhnow in a June 2005 article for the *Wall Street Journal*, it's facing a crisis because it "is running out of easy oil fields to drill" and "is barred by the Mexican constitution from tying up with foreign companies that could bring in advanced technology and help it find more oil."

Lázaro Cárdenas

This predicament flows from the founding of Pemex in 1938. The Mexican oil industry was developed in the early years of the twentieth century by British and American companies. In the mid-1930s unions representing oil workers tried to negotiate increases in wages and benefits, and the oil companies resisted. The dispute was turned over to an arbitration board that ordered a 27 percent wage hike plus new benefits, such as sick leave and vacation pay. Even though this ruling was upheld by the Mexican Supreme Court, the oil companies refused to cave.

The denouement was described by *New York Times* correspondent Alan Riding in his book *Distant Neighbors*. In a meeting with Lázaro Cárdenas, the president of Mexico, the oil companies were promised that the wage and benefit increases would not exceed $7.2 million. "I guarantee that you won't have any problems," Cárdenas told the oil companies. One of the company representatives responded: "Mr. President, those are your words. Who guarantees for you?"

"That remark," said Riding, "served to seal the companies' fate." On March 18, 1938, Cárdenas told the Mexican people in a nationwide broadcast that the 17 foreign companies were being expropriated for their "arrogant and rebellious attitude." The oil industry was nationalized, and all the companies, along with their managers, were kicked out of the country. "The oil is ours," said Cárdenas. And Pemex was born.

Pemex was a giant at its birth, and it remains a giant. The government owns it and takes 60 percent of the revenues. The ownership, established in the Mexican constitution, extends not just to the oil fields, but to refineries and every single gasoline station in the country. In 2004, Pemex paid $42 billion in taxes, one-third of the government's total tax revenue.

Corruption has been rampant in the Pemex ranks, with union leaders sharing in the spoils. Barred by the constitution from any collaboration with foreign companies, Pemex has done little to develop natural gas fields, and its refining capacity is so weak that it has to send much of its heavy crude oil to a refinery in Deer Park, Texas, that it jointly owns with Royal Dutch/Shell Group. The *Wall Street Journal* reported that Mexico spends $13 billion a year importing petroleum products while exporting $21 billion worth of oil products, resulting in prices 10 to 20 percent higher than those paid by U.S. consumers for gasoline at the pump.

Yum! Brands, based in Louisville, Kentucky, owns Pizza Hut, KFC, and Taco Bell (fast-food joints spun off by PepsiCo. in 1997), as well as Long John Silver's and A&W. It has a total of 34,000 restaurants in more than 100 countries and 256,000 employees, making Yum! the world's largest restaurant operator.

The World's Largest Family-Owned Companies

	Country	Amount owned or controlled by family members
BMW	Germany	Quandt family owns 47%
Cargill	United States	Family owns 85%
Carrefour	France	Families control 40% of shares
Fiat	Italy	Agnelli family owns 30%
Ford	United States	Ford family has 40% of voting shares
IFI	Italy	Agnelli family owns 100%
LG Group	South Korea	Koo and Huh families own 50%
Peugeot-Citroen	France	Family controls 42% of shares
Samsung	South Korea	Lee family controls 22%
Wal-Mart	United States	Walton family owns 38%

THE WORD "COFFEE" COMES FROM KAFFA, A REGION IN ETHIOPIA THAT IS BELIEVED TO BE THE ORIGIN OF COFFEE BEANS.

Coffee is grown in more than 50 countries. Brazil accounts for one-third of the world's production. After that come Vietnam, Colombia, Indonesia, India, Mexico, Ethiopa, Guatemala, Ivory Coast, and Uganda.

OF THE 500 COMPANIES ON THE FORTUNE 500 LIST IN 1981, ONLY 161 WERE STILL ON IT IN 2004.

Procter & Gamble has 18 brands that each do more than $1 billion of sales a year. They are: Actonel, Always/Whisper, Ariel, Bounty, Charmin, Crest, Downy/Lenor, Duracell, Folgers, Gillette, Head & Shoulders, Iams, Olay, Pampers, Pantene, Pringles, Tide, and Wella.

Shirt Tales

According to the World Trade Organization, this is how long it takes workers in nine different countries to make a shirt, and how much it costs to produce the shirt.

	MINUTES TO MAKE	COST FOR PRODUCTION
Northern China	**14.3**	**$0.50**
Bangladesh	**22.2**	**$0.89**
India	**22.2**	**$0.89**
Lesotho	**22.2**	**$0.89**
Vietnam	**15.4**	**$0.92**
Southern China	**12.5**	**$1.00**
Indonesia	**18.2**	**$1.09**
Sri Lanka	**20**	**$1.20**
Mexico	**30.3**	**$2.42**

Teach Your Son to Play First Base

Here are the average annual salaries of baseball players in 2004, according to position played:

First base: $6.8 million

Outfield: $4.5 million

Third base: $3.8 million

Starting pitcher: $3.7 million

Shortstop: $3.5 million

Second base: $2.9 million

Designated hitter: $2.6 million

Relief pitcher: $1.4 million

Indian Hospitality

Immigrants from India, mostly from the state of Gujarat, now own one-third of the 53,000 hotels in the United States, according to a report by Joseph Berger in the *New York Times*. The Indians have scooped up these franchises during the past 30 years, targeting the budget and mid-priced markets. They have their own association, the Asian American Hotel Owners Association, which has 8,400 members who own more than 20,000 hotels. Half the Days Inns, half the Ramadas, and 40 percent of the Holiday Inns are now believed to be in Indian hands. One company, Hersha Hospitality Trust, has gone public with a listing on the American Stock Exchange. Hersha rents 2,200 rooms in more than 20 hotels bearing names such as Comfort Inn, Fairfield Inn, Holiday Inn, and Hampton Inn.

PROFILE

Nissin Foods

TOKYO-BASED NISSIN FOODS introduced the world's first instant noodle product, Chicken Ramen, in 1958, following it up in 1971 with Cup Noodles.

The market for instant noodles has grown to more than 65 billion servings a year, with Nissin claiming first place in sales. It operates 25 factories in eight countries, including two in the United States and one in the Netherlands. This production adds up to sales of more than $3 billion a year.

The largest market for instant noodles, accounting for 40 percent of the total, is China, which Nissin entered in 2004 via a joint operation with a Chinese company, Hebei Hualong.

English is not its strong point. In Nissin's 2004 annual report, the company said it "has the status of No. 1 global share in servings sold within its sights."

African-American CEOs

Kenneth Chenault, American Express

Erroll Davis, Alliant

Ann Fudge, Young & Rubicam

Carl Horton, Absolut

Aylwin Lewis, K-mart Holdings

Bob Wood, Crompton

Renetta McCann, Starcom MediaVest Group

Stanley O'Neal, Merrill Lynch

Clarence Otis, Darden Restaurants

Richard Parsons, Time Warner

John Thompson, Symantec

Top 5 Radio Giants

	NUMBER OF STATIONS OWNED 1999	NUMBER OF STATIONS OWNED 2004
Clear Channel	512	1,270
Cumulus	232	301
Citadel	108	213
Infinity	163	180
Entercom	42	104

2003 Merchandise Sales of Fictional Characters

Mickey Mouse and friends	$5.8 billion
Winnie the Pooh and friends	$5.6 billion
Frodo Baggins (*Lord of the Rings*)	$2.9 billion
Harry Potter	$2.8 billion
Nemo (of *Finding Nemo*)	$2 billion
Yu-gi-oh	$1.8 billion
SpongeBob Square Pants	$1.5 billion
Spider-Man	$1.3 billion
Wolverine (*X-Men*)	$900 million
Pokemon	$826 million

FRATRICIDE

The Kushners

Charles Kushner

CHARLES KUSHNER inherited a New Jersey construction business founded by his father and built it into a real estate empire that controlled thousands of apartments and millions of square feet of commercial and industrial space. He also became a leading philanthropist and one of the top donors to Democratic politicians.

But along the way he became embroiled in a bitter squabble with family members over how the proceeds from the business were distributed. This dispute led to an indictment by the Justice Department for tax evasion, witness tampering, and making illegal campaign contributions. The chief witness against him was his brother-in-law.

Kushner retaliated against his brother-in-law by hiring a prostitute to seduce him, arranging to have the encounter videotaped, and then sending the tape to his sister. Kushner pleaded guilty to the charges and in March 2005 federal judge Jose L. Linares sentenced him to two years in jail, despite 700 letters from people testifying to his many charitable acts.

THE WORLD'S THREE LARGEST SELLERS OF COFFEE ARE NESTLÉ (NESCAFE), PROCTER & GAMBLE (FOLGERS), AND KRAFT (MAXWELL HOUSE). FOLGERS IS AMONG THE TOP-SELLING BRANDS IN THE U.S. MARKET, WITH 36 PERCENT OF THE GROUND COFFEE MARKET.

Gannett: Accumulator of Newspapers

Based in Rochester, New York, where it was founded in 1906 by Frank E. Gannett, the Gannett Company has assembled the largest collection of daily newspapers of any company in the world. It is expert at acquiring papers instead of starting them, although it did launch *USA Today* in 1982. By the time he died in 1957, Frank Gannett had 30 daily newspapers in his stable. Today, the company bearing his name has 103 dailies in the United States and 18 in the United Kingdom. It also publishes a dozen magazines. The roster:

ALABAMA *Montgomery Advertiser* (Montgomery) • **ARKANSAS** *The Baxter Bulletin* (Mountain Home) • **ARIZONA** *The Arizona Republic* (Phoenix), *Tucson Citizen* (Tucson) • **CALIFORNIA** *The Desert Sun* (Palm Springs), *The Salinas Californian* (Salinas), *Tulare Advance-Register* (Tulare), *Visalia Times-Delta* (Visalia) • **COLORADO** *Fort Collins Coloradoan* (Fort Collins) • **CONNECTICUT** *Norwich Bulletin* (Norwich) • **DELAWARE** *The News Journal* (Wilmington) • **FLORIDA** *Florida Today* (Brevard County), *The News-Press* (Fort Myers), *Pensacola News Journal* (Pensacola) • **GUAM** *Hagatna Pacific Daily News* • **HAWAII** *The Honolulu Advertiser* (Honolulu) • **IDAHO** *The Idaho Statesman* (Boise) • **ILLINOIS** *Rockford Register Star* (Rockford) • **INDIANA** *The Indianapolis Star* (Indianapolis), *Journal and Courier* (Lafayette), *Chronicle-Tribune* (Marion), *The Star Press* (Muncie), *Palladium-Item* (Richmond) • **IOWA** *The Des Moines Register* (Des Moines), *Iowa City Press-Citizen* (Iowa City) • **KENTUCKY** *The Courier-Journal* (Louisville) • **LOUISIANA** *Alexandria Daily Town Talk* (Alexandria), *The Daily Advertiser* (Lafayette), *The News-Star* (Monroe), *Daily World* (Opelousas), *The Times* (Shreveport) • **MARYLAND** *The Daily Times* (Salisbury) • **MICHIGAN** *Battle Creek Enquirer* (Battle Creek), *The Detroit News* (Detroit), *The Detroit News and Free Press* (Detroit), *Lansing State Journal* (Lansing), *Times Herald* (Port Huron) • **MINNESOTA** *St. Cloud Times* (St. Cloud) • **MISSOURI** *Springfield News-Leader* (Springfield) • **MISSISSIPPI** *Hattiesburg American* (Hattiesburg), *The Clarion-Ledger* (Jackson) • **MONTANA** *Great Falls Tribune* (Great Falls) • **NEVADA** *Reno Gazette-Journal* (Reno) • **NEW JERSEY** *Asbury Park Press* (Asbury Park), *Courier News* (Bridgewater), *Courier-Post* (Cherry Hill), *Home News Tribune* (East Brunswick), *Daily Record* (Morristown), *The Daily Journal* (Vineland) • **NEW MEXICO** *Alamogordo Daily News**

(Alamogordo), *Carlsbad Current-Argus** (Carlsbad), *The Deming Headlight** (Deming), *The Daily Times** (Farmington), *Las Cruces Sun-News** (Las Cruces), *Silver City Sun-News** (Silver City) • **NEW YORK** *Press & Sun-Bulletin* (Binghamton), *Star-Gazette* (Elmira), *The Ithaca Journal* (Ithaca), *Poughkeepsie Journal* (Poughkeepsie), *Rochester Democrat and Chronicle* (Rochester), *Observer-Dispatch* (Utica), *The Journal News* (Westchester County) • **NORTH CAROLINA** *Asheville Citizen-Times* (Asheville) • **OHIO** *Telegraph-Forum* (Bucyrus), *Chillicothe Gazette* (Chillicothe), *The Cincinnati Enquirer* (Cincinnati), *Coshocton Tribune* (Coshocton), *The News-Messenger* (Fremont), *Lancaster Eagle-Gazette* (Lancaster), *News Journal* (Mansfield), *The Marion Star* (Marion), *The Advocate* (Newark), *News Herald* (Port Clinton), *Times Recorder* (Zanesville) • **OKLAHOMA** *Muskogee Daily Phoenix* (Muskogee) • **OREGON** *Statesman Journal* (Salem) • **PENNSYLVANIA** *Public Opinion* (Chambersburg) • **SOUTH CAROLINA** *The Greenville News* (Greenville) • **SOUTH DAKOTA** *Argus Leader* (Sioux Falls) • **TENNESSEE** *The Leaf-Chronicle* (Clarksville), *The Review Appeal* (Franklin), *The Jackson Sun* (Jackson), *Daily News Journal* (Murfreesboro), *The Tennessean* (Nashville) • **TEXAS** *El Paso Times** (El Paso) • **UTAH** *The Spectrum* (St. George) • **VERMONT** *The Burlington Free Press* (Burlington) • **VIRGINIA** *The Daily News Leader* (Staunton) • **WASHINGTON** *The Bellingham Herald* (Bellingham), *The Olympian* (Olympia) • **WISCONSIN** *The Post-Crescent* (Appleton), *The Reporter* (Fond du Lac), *Green Bay Press-Gazette* (Green Bay), *Herald Times Reporter* (Manitowoc), *Marshfield News-Herald* (Marshfield), *Oshkosh Northwestern* (Oshkosh), *The Sheboygan Press* (Sheboygan), *Central Wisconsin Sunday* (Stevens Point), *Stevens Point Journal* (Stevens Point), *Wausau Daily Herald* (Wausau), *The Daily Tribune* (Wisconsin Rapids) • **WEST VIRGINIA** *The Herald-Dispatch* (Huntington)

*Published by Texas–New Mexico Newspapers Partnership. Gannett has 66.2 percent interest.

MAGAZINES OWNED BY GANNETT:

USA Weekend • *Army Times* • *Navy Times* • *Marin Corps Times* • *Air Force Times* • *Federal Times* • *Defense News* • *Armed Forces Journal* • *C4ISR Journal* • *Training and Simulation Journal* • *Clipper Magazine* • *Nursing Spectrum* (including *NurseWeek*)

UK NEWSPAPERS OWNED BY GANNETT:

Bolton Evening News, Bolton • *Daily Echo*, Bournemouth • *Dorset Echo*, Weymouth • *Sindon Evening Advertiser*, Swindon • *The Argus*, Brighton • *Basildon/Southend Evening Echo*, Basildon • *Colchester Evening Gazette*, Cochester • *Evening Press*, York • *Lancashire Evening Telegraph*, Blackburn • *The Northern Echo*, Darlington • *Oxford Mail*, Oxford • *South Wales Argus*, Newport • *Southern Daily Echo*, Southampton • *Bradford Telegraph & Argus*, Bradford • *Worcester Evening News*, Worcester • *The Herald*, Glasgow • *Evening Times*, Glasgow • *Sunday Herald*, Glasgow

Avis: The Most Sold and Resold Company in American Business History

1946 Avis founded by Warren Avis at Detroit's Willow Run Airport.

1954 Avis sold to Boston financier Richard Robie for $8 million.

1956 Avis acquired by investment group led by Amoskeag Company.

1962 Investment banker Lazard Frères buys Avis.

1965 ITT buys Avis for $51 million.

1972 ITT spins off Avis as a public company.

1977 Avis acquired by Norton Simon Inc. for $174 million.

1983 Avis becomes part of Esmark as a result of company's $1 billion purchase of Norton Simon.

1984 Avis becomes part of Beatrice Foods when Beatrice acquires Esmark for $2.5 billion.

1986 Investment firm Kohlberg, Kravis, Roberts acquires Beatrice for $6.2 billion in leveraged buyout.

1986 Investment firm Wesray Capital acquires Avis from Beatrice for $263 million plus assumption of debt.

1987 Avis acquired by the Avis Employee Stock Ownership Plan for $750 million plus assumption of debt, making Avis the largest employee-owned company in the United States.

1989 General Motors becomes a minority stockholder in Avis.

1996 Avis acquired by HFS Inc., world's largest franchiser of hotels and real estate brokerage houses.

1997 Avis becomes a public company again.

2001 Cendant, owner of HFS, acquires all the shares of Avis that it did not already own for $937 million.

Major Appliance* Brands in the U.S. Market

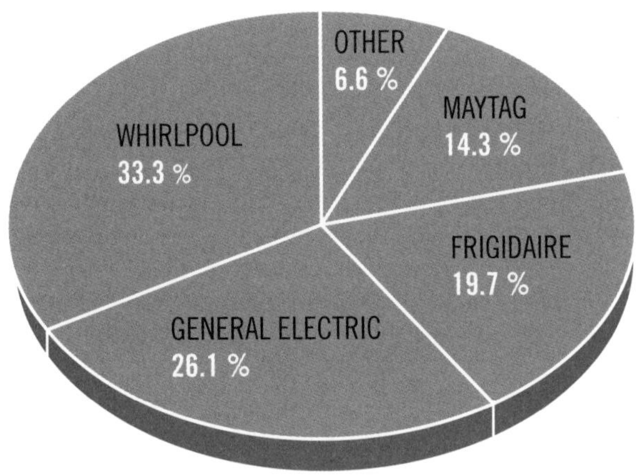

**Dishwashers, washing machines, dryers, freezers, ranges, refrigerators*

General Electric, School for CEOs

When American companies look for a new CEO, a very likely source is General Electric, known as a great training ground for leaders. Here are 11 CEOs who are GE alumni:

Bob Nardelli, Home Depot
Larry Johnston, Albertsons
David Cote, Honeywell
Jim McNerney, 3M
Kevin Sharer, Amgen
Peter Cartwright, Calpine
Christopher Kearney, SPX
Matt Espe, IKON
Mark Frissora, Tenneco Automotive
Barry Perry, Engelhard
Dan Mudd, Fannie Mae

PROFILE

Mars

CANDY MAKER FRANK MARS of Minneapolis, Minnesota, introduced the Milky Way candy bar in 1923, followed by Snickers in 1930 and 3 Musketeers in 1937. Now the Mars company is a giant corporation, headquartered in McLean, Virginia, near the CIA, another secretive outfit. Descendants of Frank Mars own the company entirely, have nothing to do with the stock market, and don't entertain inquiries from the press. Their annual sales are estimated at $20 billion, making them the third largest private company in the United States. They also have a formidable presence in Britain. They make the world's bestselling candy, M&Ms. And they also make a bunch of other products, including Uncle Ben's rice and the pet foods Kal Kan, Pedigree, Sheba, and Waltham's.

FRATRICIDE

The Koch family

THE FOUR KOCH BROTHERS—Fred, Charles, William, and David—each inherited millions of dollars from the company founded by their father, Fred. Based in Wichita, Kansas, Koch Industries ranks as the second largest privately held company in the United States. Originally an oil refiner, it's now into all kinds of things: asphalt, chemicals, cattle, and finance, to name just a few (see page 13).

Meanwhile, as the company grew, the brothers carried on a slugfest that lasted more than 20 years. William, who lives in Palm Beach, Florida, in a 36,000-square-foot (3,300 sq m) mansion, joined with his older brother, Fred, in suing their two other brothers about deals to sell company stock. Along the way, in 1981, William also sued his 82-year-old mother, forcing her to take the witness stand shortly after suffering a stroke. The brothers say they finally settled their differences in 2002, ending the dispute.

William Koch has had an active life. A chemical engineer with three degrees from MIT, he founded and still owns Oxbow, North America's largest exporter of petroleum coke. In 1992 he spent $66 million to win the America's Cup. He has fathered children inside and outside his two marriages. He is also a major collector of antiques and paintings. In an interview with the *New York Times* in 2004, William said: "My brother Charles collects money. David used to collect girls, but not anymore. Fred collects castles. And I collect everything."

COSMOPOLITAN MAGAZINE HAS MORE INTERNATIONAL EDITIONS THAN ANY OTHER PERIODICAL, AT 55.

PROFILE

Green Bay Packers

IT'S LOVE, NOT MONEY, that has motivated football fans to buy shares in the Green Bay Packers. Some 111,500 people own 4,748,910 shares. The stock is not listed on any exchange. No dividends are ever paid. Stockholders have no season ticket privileges. The stock has no chance of appreciating in value. And it cannot be resold, except back to the team for a fraction of the original price. Yet the team has had no trouble attracting buyers who want to be part owners of the Wisconsin football club.

In its first four years, 1919–22, the team had three owners. It called itself the "Packers" because of the first owner, Indian Packing Company. In 1923, it became a community-owned team, selling 1,000 shares at $5 apiece to Green Bay residents. The shareholders also had to commit to at least six season tickets.

In 1935, after going into receivership, the company was reorganized, raising $15,000 through the sale of 300 shares. In 1950, after the departure of longtime coach and founder Curly Lambeau, the company's bylaws were amended to permit the issuance of up to 10,000 shares of stock. The stock was priced at $25 a share, and the sale was opened to Wisconsin residents and former Green Bay residents living in other states. This sale raised $118,000.

The fourth drive, to raise money for redevelopment of Lambeau Field, came in 1997. Now the sale of stock, at $200 a share, was open to everyone in the United States. There was a stampede for the stock. During the early weeks, orders poured into Green Bay at the rate of 3,500 a day. By the end of the 17-week drive, the club had raised more than $24 million—and the number of shareholders had jumped from 1,940 to more than 100,000. More than half of the new shares (64,300) were bought by Wisconsin residents, followed by Illinois (9,600), Minnesota (4,300), California (3,700), Florida (2,900), Michigan (2,800), Texas (2,500), and Ohio (2,000).

Bylaws specifically prohibit any individual from holding more than 200,000 shares. They also state that if the club is ever sold, all the monies, after expenses, would go not to the shareholders but to the nonprofit Green Bay Packers Foundation.

Top Users of Corporate Jets for Personal Travel in 2004

	COMPANY	VALUE OF BENEFIT
1. Barry Diller	IAC/Interactive	$832,000
2. Joseph Steinberg	Leucadia	$744,000*
3. C. John Wilder	TXU	$561,000
4. Dennis Dammerman	General Electric	$504,000
5. Philip Purcell	Morgan Stanley	$467,000
6. Robert Rubin	Citicorp	$459,000
7. Tracy Krohn	W&T Offshore	$406,000
8. James Dimon	JPMorgan Chase	$395,000*
9. Michael Jeffries	Abercrombie & Fitch	$361,000
10. Jay Fishman	St. Paul Travelers	$361,000
11. Margaret Whitman	eBay	$358,000*
12. William Harrison	JPMorgan Chase	$354,000*

**Includes payment by company to cover taxes on plane usage*

FRATRICIDE

The Mondavis

CESARE MONDAVI, a grape grower, bought the historic Charles Krug winery in California's Napa Valley in 1943, turning it over to his two sons, Peter and Robert, to run. The brothers had different personalities—Peter, conservative, not open to change, Robert, sophisticated and daring, looking to expand the business. These differences resulted in a fist fight in 1965, after which Robert walked out and went down the road to open a new winery under his own name. It was a highly successful venture, with Robert Mondavi rising to become the sixth largest winery in the United States, with a stock market listing on NASDAQ.

Robert Mondavi

Robert's two sons, Timothy and Michael, went to work for the winery right after graduating from college. They eventually served as co-CEOs. However, sibling rivalry also erupted in the second generation. The brothers clashed repeatedly over the winery's business strategy. They were also on opposite sides of the fence about whether to sell stock to the public.

In the early years of the twenty-first century, financial results were poor. Timothy left the company in 2003. Mondavi's share price slid from $40 to $18 in 2003. In 2004, Michael was replaced as chairman, and he was asked to leave the board after opposing a plan to reorganize the company into two divisions, one that sold high-end wines like Opus and Robert Mondavi Reserve, and one that focused on wines selling under $15 a bottle.

Toward the end of 2004, the strife-torn company was sold to New York–based Constellation Brands, the largest wine producer in the country, for $1 billion. Robert Mondavi will continue to serve as ambassador for the brand that bears his name. His two sons each received $1 million in severance and 50 free cases of wine a year.

TOP 10

Wealthiest Europeans*

(Excluding the UK)

1. **Albrecht family** (Aldi Supermarkets)	Germany	$33.7 (£17.7) billion
2. **Ingvar Kamprad** (IKEA)	Sweden	$22.9 (£12) billion
3. **Quandt family** (BMW)	Germany	$20.2 (£10.6) billion
4. **Liliane Bettencourt** (L'Oréal)	France	$17 (£8.9) billion
5. **Bernard Arnault** (LVMH—Moët Hennessy, Louis Vuitton, Fendi, Dom Pérignon)	France	$16.8 (£8.8) billion
6. **Brenninkmeyer family** (C&A fashion stores)	Netherlands	$15.8 (£8.3) billion
7. **Amancio Ortega** (Zara)	Spain	$12.6 (£6.6) billion
8. **Stefan Persson** (H&M)	Sweden	$12.4 (£6.5) billion
9. **Silvio Berlusconi** (media)	Italy	$11.8 (£6.2) billion
10. **Oeri-Hoffmann family** (Roche)	Switzerland	$11 (£5.8) billion

**2005 ranking by the* Sunday Times *of London*

Two brothers from Illinois, Charles and George Page, went to Switzerland after the American Civil War and set up a dairy company. Their company later combined with a similar company set up by a German-born Swiss businessman, Henri Nestlé, to form what became the world's largest food company: Nestlé.

TOP 10 SELLING

Passenger Cars in the United States

	1981	1989	2004
1.	Chevette (GM)	Honda Accord	Toyota Camry
2.	Chevy Citation	Ford Taurus	Honda Accord
3.	Ford Escort	Ford Escort	Honda Civic
4.	Olds Cutlass	Corsica/Beretta (GM)	Chevy Impala
5.	Toyota Corolla	Chevy Cavalier	Toyota Corolla
6.	Chevy Malibu	Toyota Camry	Chevy Malibu
7.	Chevrolet	Honda Civic	Ford Taurus
8.	Buick Regal	Ford Tempo	Nissan Altima
9.	Buick Skylark	Nissan Sentra	Ford Focus
10.	Reliant/Volare (Chrysler)	Grand Am (GM)	Chevy Cavalier

The Food Revolution in America

	1994	2004
Number of farmers' markets	1,755	3,137
Number of certified organic farms	4,050	11,998
Number of FDA-approved bioengineered foods	1	54
Number of cooking schools	338	930
Total sales of restaurant food	$281.5 billion	$440.1 billion
Total sales of bottled water	$3.4 billion	$6.7 billion
Olive oil sales (metric tons)	115,000	190,000
Dry pasta sales	$1.7 billion	$2.0 billion
Total value of imported wine	$1 billion	$3.2 billion
Percentage of adults who are vegetarian	1	2.8

THE WORLD'S BESTSELLING PERFUME, CHANEL NO. 5, WAS INTRODUCED BY GABRIELLE "COCO" CHANEL IN 1921. SHE NAMED IT AFTER HER FAVORITE NUMBER, INTRODUCING IT TO THE WORLD ON THE FIFTH DAY OF THE FIFTH MONTH, MAY.

♦ ♦ ♦ FRATRICIDE ♦ ♦ ♦

The Ambanis

RELIANCE INDUSTRIES is India's largest private sector company, a leader in petrochemicals, cell phones, and energy exploration. After the founder, Dhirubhai Ambani, died in 2002 without leaving a will, warfare broke out between his two sons, Mukesh and Anil. Anil, the younger brother, charged that Mukesh had illegally seized control of the company, freezing him out. India's finance minister, P. Chidambaram, urged the feuding brothers to settle their differences. Reports in the Indian press said that at a family meeting, the brothers had agreed to abide by a decision reached by their mother, Kokilaben Ambani. The family owns 34 percent of Reliance, which is valued at $17 billion.

The Demise of British-Owned Car Makers

In 2005, when the Rover car company ran out of gas, it marked the end of British-owned automobile manufacturers, except for small boutique companies such as Morgan. Cars are still made in the United Kingdom, but their producers are all foreign companies—American, French, German, and Japanese. All the major British car companies have either disappeared or—like Bentley, Jaguar, and Rolls-Royce—passed into foreign hands. It's a far cry from the 1920s, the heyday of British auto manufacturing. During that decade, 288 different car models were turned out by British-owned companies.

Selected Sources

p. 12, "Ratio of CEO Pay to Average Worker Pay": United for a Fair Economy

p. 12, "Golden Age of Film": *New Yorker*

p. 14, "Average Age of Car Owners": J.D. Power and Associates

p. 17, "Prices of Sought-After First English Language Editions in the Rare Book Trade": Loblolly Books, Ralph Sipper/Books

pp. 18–19: Russell Investment Group, Tacoma, Washington

p. 25, "Ah, Those Golden Years": *New York Times*

p. 26, "Top 10 Donors to K–12 Education": Manhattan Institute

p. 33, "Average Paychecks of Workers in New York City in 2004": Adams Beverage Group

p. 41, "Top 10 U.S. Philanthropists": *Forbes*

pp. 42–43: Russell Investment Group, London

p. 48, "10 Best Workplaces in the United Kingdom, 2005": *Financial Times*, Great Place to Work Institute—UK

p. 50, "10 Largest Employers in New York City": *Crain's New York Business*

p. 51, "10 Largest Employers in Douglas County, Kansas": Lawrence, Kansas, Chamber of Commerce

pp. 54–55: Russell Investment Group, Tacoma, Washington

p. 58, "World's 50 Largest Companies": Forbes

p. 60: "Top Selling Liquor Brands in the United States": Adams Beverage Group

p. 62: "General Electric, Relentless Shopper": *Financial Times*

p. 65: "Top 10 Places to Work in the United States": Great Place to Work Institute, *Fortune*

pp. 72–73: "How Companies Divided Their Political Contributions in the 2004 U.S. Election": Center for Responsive Politics

pp. 74–75: Russell Investment Group, London

pp. 76–77: "Top 25 Soccer Teams": *Forbes*

p. 79: "Top 10 Richest Americans": *Forbes*

p. 80: "World's 15 Largest Employers": *Fortune*

p. 83: "Drugs Around the World": IMS Health

pp. 84–85: Russell Investment Group, Tacoma, Washington

p. 86–87: "World's Top 50 Restaurants": *Restaurant* magazine

pp. 90–91: Russell Investment Group, London

p. 93: "Changing Advertising Mix": Universal McCann

p. 96: "Top CEO Golfers": *Golf Digest*

p. 97: "Top 10 Richest Residents of the UK": *Sunday Times* of London

p. 101: "Top 20 Companies for New College Graduates": *The Black Collegian*

pp. 102–103: Russell Investment Group, Tacoma, Washington

p. 104: "Top 50 Companies Recognized for Diversity": *Diversity Inc.*

pp. 106–109, "All-Time Worldwide Box Office Rankings": imdb.com

p. 113, "10 Largest Private Companies in the United States": *Forbes*

p. 116, "Millions of Millionaires": Capgemini/Merrill Lynch World Wealth Report 2005

p. 118, "Top 13 Pharmaceutical Companies": IMS Health

p. 119, "How Long Does It Take Automakers to Build a Car?": Harbor Report

pp. 122–123: Russell Investment Group, London

p. 129: "Who Buys the Most Insurance?": World Trade Organization

p. 132: "The World's Largest Family-Owned Companies": *Family Business*

p. 133: "Shirt Tales": World Trade Organization

p. 136: "2003 Merchandise Sales of Fictional Characters": *Forbes*

p. 147: "Top 10 Wealthiest Europeans": *Sunday Times* of London

p. 149: "The Food Revolution in America": *Saveur*

Index

Numbers in **bold** indicate illustrations

Acknowledgments

Having dealt with this kind of information all my working life, I need to pay tribute to my early mentors: the late John Crichton and the late Jarlath Graham, both editors in chief of the trade journal *Advertising Age*, where I first learned to write about business. Two others who had great influence on me were the market researcher Alfred Politz and the advertising executive Norman Strouse, also both deceased. Theodore L. Cross, an extraordinary publisher, has been a sounding board and counselor for me for the past 35 years.

This is one of the few books I wrote without the collaboration of Robert Levering, but he was an enthusiastic fan of this collection—and his encouragement meant a great deal to me. I want to thank the following for their contributions: Andrew Lawrence, Shelley Alpern, John Stokes, Michael Katz, the three Townsend brothers—Laird, Lee, and Blaine—and my thoughtful son, Eben, as well as my daughter-in-law, Leigh Ann Townsend. My daughter, Abigail, was an unfailing source of support for this project at all its stages, and she made suggestions that were enormously helpful.

A book of this kind desperately needed a dogged researcher, and I was fortunate to have one in Mariko Fujinaka. She tracked down countless items, filled in gaps, and made dry statistics come alive. The stock market lists resulted from analyses by the talented people at Russell Investment Group: Mahesh Pritamani in Tacoma, and Tom Goodwin and Joo Hee Lee in London.

Every writer should have an agent like Joy Tutela at the David Black Literary Agency. She was a tireless advocate of the book, and she found a home for it at Quirk Books, where Melissa Wagner did a superb job of editing all the statistical salvos thrown at her.

My thanks also to Ben Schott, whose miscellany books inspired me to put this collection together.

Finally, my greatest debt is to Elizabeth Campbell Rollins, who consented to be my bride midway through this publishing adventure. Her optimism and joie de vivre make all goals seem attainable.